George Franklin Edmunds, United States Congress Senate

Report on the Letter from the Attorney-General

declining to transmit to the Senate copies of official records and papers

concerning the administration of the office of the district attorney of the

southern district of Alabama

George Franklin Edmunds, United States Congress Senate

Report on the Letter from the Attorney-General
declining to transmit to the Senate copies of official records and papers concerning the administration of the office of the district attorney of the southern district of Alabama

ISBN/EAN: 9783337170585

Printed in Europe, USA, Canada, Australia, Japan

Cover: Foto ©Suzi / pixelio.de

More available books at **www.hansebooks.com**

IN THE SENATE OF THE UNITED STATES.

FEBRUARY 18, 1886.—Ordered to be printed.

Mr. EDMUNDS, from the Committee on the Judiciary, submitted the following

REPORT

ON THE

The Committee on the Judiciary, to which was referred a letter from the Attorney-General of the United States declining to transmit to the Senate copies of official records and papers concerning the administration of the office of district attorney of the southern district of Alabama from January 1, 1885, to January 25, 1886, respectfully reports :

That on the 17th of July, 1885, the President of the United States, pursuant to the provisions of section 1768 the Revised Statutes, suspended George M. Duskin from the execution of the duties of the office of district attorney of said district, by an order in the following words:

> EXECUTIVE MANSION,
> *Washington, D.C., July 17, 1885.*
>
> SIR: You are hereby suspended from the office of attorney of the United States for the southern district of Alabama, in accordance with the terms of section 1768, Revised Statutes of the United States, and subject to all provisions of law applicable thereto.
>
> GROVER CLEVELAND.
>
> To GEORGE M. DUSKIN, Esq.,
> *United States Attorney, Mobile, Ala.*

And on the same day, pursuant to the same statute, designated John D. Burnett to perform the duties of such suspended officer in the mean time, by a letter of authority in the words following:

> *Grover Cleveland, President of the United States of America, to all who shall see these presents, greeting :*
>
> Know ye, that by virtue of the authority conferred upon the President by section 1768 of the Revised Statutes of the United States, I do hereby suspend George M. Duskin, of Alabama, from the office of attorney of the United States for the southern district of Alabama, until the end of the next session of the Senate; and I hereby designate John D. Burnett of Alabama, to perform the duties of such suspended offi

cer in the mean time, he being a suitable person therefor; subject to all provisions of law applicable thereto.

In testimony whereof I have caused these letters to be made patent, and the seal of the United States to be hereunto affixed.

Given under my hand at the city of Washington, the seventeenth day of July, in the year of our Lord one thousand eight hundred and eighty-five, and of the Independence of the United States of America the one hundred and tenth.

GROVER CLEVELAND.

By the President:

[SEAL.]

T. F. BAYARD,
Secretary of State.

On the 14th December, 1885, the Senate then being in session, the President nominated the same John D. Burnett to be attorney of the United States for the southern district of Alabama in the place of the said Duskin, suspended, in the following words:

> I nominate John D. Burnett, of Alabama, to be attorney of the United States for the southern district of Alabama, vice George M. Duskin, suspended.

GROVER CLEVELAND.

This nomination was in due course referred to the Committee on the Judiciary.

Since the passage of the act of 2d March, 1867, "regarding the tenure of certain civil offices," it has been the practice of the Committee on the Judiciary, whenever a nomination has been made proposing the removal from office of one person and the appointment of another, to address a note to the head of the Department having such matters in charge (usually the Attorney General), asking that all papers and information in the possession of the Department touching the conduct and administration of the officer proposed to be removed, and touching the character and conduct of the person proposed to be appointed, be sent to the committee for its information. This practice has through all administrations been carried on with the unanimous approval of all the members of the committee, although the composition of the committee has been during this period sometimes of one political character and sometimes of another. In no instance until this time has the committee met with any delay or denial in respect of furnishing such papers and information, with a single exception, and in which exception the delay and suggested denial lasted for only two or three days.

The committee has thus hitherto been enabled to know the character and quality of the administration of the office in charge of the incumbent proposed to be removed as well as the character and quality of the person proposed to be appointed, so far as the papers in the Department could furnish information in regard thereto.

In the instance now particularly under consideration, the committee, according to its standing course, on December 26, 1885, through its chairman, addressed a note to the Attorney-General in the same form, and asking for the same papers and information, that it had been accustomed to do. After sundry delays and explanations it became evident to the committee that it could not by this informal method obtain an inspection of the papers and documents in the Department of Justice bearing upon the subject. It accordingly, on the 25th of January, 1886, reported to the Senate, for its adoption, a resolution in the following words:

> *Resolved,* That the Attorney-General of the United States be, and he hereby is, directed to transmit to the Senate copies of all documents and papers that have been filed in the Department of Justice since the 1st day of January, A. D. 1885, in relation to the management and conduct of the office of district attorney of the United States of the southern district of Alabama.

which on the next day was adopted by the Senate without a division.

The Attorney-General, on the 1st day of February, 1886, sent to the Senate a communication in the following words:

DEPARTMENT OF JUSTICE,
January 28, 1886.

The President pro tempore of the Senate of the United States:

I acknowledge the receipt of a resolution of the Senate adopted on the 25th instant, in executive session as follows:"

"*Resolved,* That the Attorney-General of the United States be, and he hereby is, directed to transmit to the Senate copies of all documents and papers that have been filed in the Department of Justice since the 1st day of January, A. D. 1885, in relation to the management and conduct of the office of district attorney of the United States of the southern district of Alabama."

In response to the said resolution the President of the United States directs me to say that the papers which were in this Department relating to the fitness of John D. Burnett, recently nominated to said office, having been already sent to the Judiciary Committee of the Senate, and the papers and documents which are mentioned in the said resolution, and still remaining in the custody of this Department, having exclusive reference to the suspension by the President of George M. Duskin, the late incumbent of the office of district attorney of the United States for the southern district of Alabama, it is not considered that the public interest will be promoted by a compliance with said resolution and the transmission of the papers and documents therein mentioned to the Senate in executive session.

Very respectfully, your obedient servant.

A. H. GARLAND,
Attorney-General.

This letter, although in response to the direction of the Senate that copies of any papers bearing on the subject within a given period of time be transmitted, assumes that the Attorney-General of the United States is the servant of the President, and is to give or withhold copies of documents in his office according to the will of the Executive, and not otherwise.

Your committee is unable to discover, either in the original act of 1789 creating the office of Attorney-General, or in the act of 1870 creating the Department of Justice, any provision which makes the Attorney-General of the United States in any sense the servant of or controlled by the Executive in the performance of the duties imputed to him by law or the nature of his office. It is true that in the creation of the Department of State, of War, and of the Navy it was provided in substance that these Secretaries should perform such duties as should from time to time be enjoined upon them by the President, and should conduct the business of their Departments in such manner as the President should direct, but the committee does not think it important to the main question under consideration that such direction is not to be found in the statute creating the Department of Justice, for it is thought it must be obvious that the authority intrusted by the statute in these cases to the President to direct and control the performance of duties was only a superintending authority to regulate the performance of the duties that the *law* required, and not to require the performance of duties that the laws had not devolved upon the heads of Departments, and not to dispense with or forbid the performance of such duties according as it might suit the discretion or the fancy of the Executive. The Executive is bound by the Constitution and by his oath to take care that the laws be faithfully executed, and he is himself as much bound by the regulations of law as the humblest officer in the service of the United States, and he cannot have authority to undertake to faithfully execute the laws whether applied to his own special functions or those of the Departments created by law, otherwise than by causing, so far as he lawfully may, and by lawful methods, the heads of Departments and other officers of the United States to do the duties which the law, and not his will, has imputed to them.

The important question, then is, whether it is within the constitutional competence of either house of Congress to have access to the official papers and documents in the various public offices of the United States created by laws enacted by themselves. It may be fully admitted that except in resp ct of the Department of the Treasury there is no statute which commands the head of any Department to transmit to either house of Congress on its demand any information whatever concerning the administration of his Department, but the committee believes it to be clear that from the very nature of the powers entrusted by the Constitution to the two houses of Congress, it is a necessary incident that either house must have at all times the right to know all that officially exists or takes place in any of the Departments of the Government. So perfectly was this proposition understood before and at the time of the formation of the Constitution that the Continental Congress, before the adoption of the present Constitution, in establishing a Department of Foreign Affairs and providing for a principal officer thereof, thought it fit to enact that all books, records, and other papers in that office should be open to the inspection of any *member* of Congress, provided that no copy should be taken of matters of secret nature, without special leave of Congress. . It was not thought necessary to enact that the Congress itself should be entitled to the production and inspection of such papers, for that right was supposed to exist in the very nature of things, and when under the Constitution, the Department came to be created, although the provision that each individual member of Congress should have access to the papers was omitted (evidently for reasons that can now be quite well understood), it was not thought necessary that an affirmative provision should be inserted, giving to the houses of Congress the right to know the contents of the public papers and records in the public offices of the country whose laws and whose offices they were to assist in creating.

It is believed that there is no instance of civilized governments having bodies representative of the people or of states in which the right and the power of those representative bodies to obtain in one form or another complete information as to every paper and transaction in any of the executive departments thereof does not exist, even though such papers might relate to what is ordinarily an executive function, if that function impinged upon any duty or function of the representative bodies.

A qualification of this general right may under our Constitution exist in case of calls by the House of Representatives for papers relating to treaties, &c., under consideration and not yet disposed of by the President and Senate.

The committee feels authorized to state, after a somewhat careful research, that within the foregoing limits there is scarcely in the history of this Government until now any instance of a refusal by a head of a Department, or even of the President himself, to communicate official facts and information, as distinguished from private and unofficial papers, motions, views, reasons, and opinions, to either house of Congress when unconditionally demanded. Indeed, the early journals of the Senate show great numbers of instances of directions to the heads of Departments, as of course, to furnish papers and reports upon all sorts of affairs, both legislative and executive.

The instances of requests to the President, and commands to the heads of Departments, by each house of Congress, from those days until now, for papers and information on every conceivable subject of public affairs are almost innumerable, for it appears to have been thought by all the Presidents who have carried on the Government now for almost a century, that, even in respect of requests to them, an independent and co-ordinate branch of the Government, they were under a constitutional duty and obligation to furnish to either house the papers called for—unless, as has happened in very rare instances, when the request was coupled with an appeal to the discretion of the President in respect of the danger of publicity, to send the papers if, in his judgment, it should not be incompatible with the public welfare.

Even in times of the highest party excitement and stress, as in 1826 and 1844, it did not seem to occur to the Chief Executive of the United States that it was possible that any official facts or information existing, either in the Departments created by law or within his own possession, could, save as before stated, be withheld from either of the houses of Congress, although such facts or information sometimes involved very intricate and delicate matters of foreign affairs, as well as sometimes the history and conduct of officers connected with the administration of affairs. Thus, in 1826, when the Senate thought fit to pass a resolution that, in considering whether the United States should be represented in the Congress of Panama, the Senate ought to act with open doors, unless the publication of the documents referred to in debate would be prejudicial to existing negotiations, and that the President be requested to inform the Senate whether such objection existed to the publication of the documents communicated by the Executive, and, if so, to specify the parts which would for that reason be objectionable, the President replied that all the communications had been made to the Senate in confidence and proceeded to say, "Believing that the established free confidential communication between the Executive and the Senate ought for the public interest to be preserved unimpaired, I deem it my indispensable duty to leave to the Senate itself the decision of the question involving a departure hitherto, so far as I am informed, without example, from that usage, and upon the motions for which, not being informed of them, I do not feel myself competent to decide." And although in this instance there was no question in regard to the furnishing documents or papers, and the question was merely whether the Executive was bound to give an opinion to the Senate in such a case, twenty out of forty-four Senators present appear to have voted on the yeas and nays for the proposition that the President in such a case was bound to give such an opinion to the Senate. Among those twenty were Senators Benton, Cobb, Dickerson, Hayne, King, Macon, Randolph, Van Buren, and Woodbury; and by a vote of 27 to 16 the Senate declared that it had "the right to publish communications so made and discuss the same with open doors without the consent of the President when in their opinion the public interest may require such publication and such discussion."

In 1842 the House of Representatives charged the select committee to inquire into the cause, manner, and circumstances of the removal of one St. Sylvester, late a clerk in the Pension Office, with power to send for persons and papers. On the 27th of July, 1842, Mr. Garrett Davis reported to the House upon the subject, stating that the committee had requested the Secretary to furnish for its use a copy of the charges against Sylvester and a copy of the order dismissing him and copies of any other papers in the Department touching his removal. He quotes from the response of the Secretary as follows:

The letter dismissing Mr. Sylvester was made a public record of the Department, and I therefore transmit a copy of it herewith, agreeable to your request. There is no other paper of the description specified in your request or relating to the subject on the files of this Department, nor is there any in my possession which is not of a confidential character. The faithful discharge of the duties devolving upon heads of Departments frequently renders it of essential importance to preserve confidential communications they have received as such, and private honor as well as public policy forbids that a pledge thus given should be violated.

Everything in the files was produced without question. The House adjourned soon after this report, and no final action was taken upon the subject. This report is so valuable as a discussion of the general questions connected with patronage that the committee thinks it fit to append it to this report (Appendix B). It will be seen in this instance that there was no attempt on the part of the Secretary to deny the right of the House to have the inspection of all papers in the files of the Department, but he only put himself upon the ground that private and confidential communications that were not on the files of the Department ought not to be disclosed. On the 18th May, 1844, the Senate, in executive session, adopted a resolution directing the Secretary of the Treasury to communicate whether any and what sums of money had been drawn from the Treasury to carry into effect the orders of the War and Navy Departments, made since the 12th April of that year, for increasing the military force on the frontiers of Texas, &c. On 28th of same month President Tyler sent a message to the Senate, stating that the Secretary had communicated the Senate resolution to him. He then says:

While I cannot recognize this call thus made on the head of the Department as consistent with the constitutional rights of the Senate when acting in its executive capacity, which in such case can only properly hold correspondence with the President of the United States, nevertheless, from an anxious desire to lay before the Senate all such information as may be necessary to enable it, with full understanding, to act upon any subject which may be before it, I herewith transmit communications which have been made to me by the Secretaries of War and Navy Departments in full answer to the resolution of the Senate.

In this instance it will be seen that there is no intimation of a denial of the right of either house of Congress, in the exercise of its general jurisdiction, to have knowledge of papers in and acts of a department of the Government, but only a claim that when such papers are wanted in the " executive capacity" of the Senate they ought to be called for from the President direct. It must be supposed that President Tyler was ignorant of the fact that such commands to heads of Departments had been made by the Senate continuously from the foundation of the Government down to that time, and that those commands had been obeyed, or else he must have supposed that an unbroken and unchanged practice of the Senate, under the Constitution, for more than half a century, had been under a plainly erroneous impression of its rights, not only by itself, but by the executive departments of the Government. It would seem to be too clear for argument, that whether the Senate chooses to conduct its business with closed doors or open doors, is a matter entirely for its consideration and can have no relation to the obligation of the executive departments of the Government to respond to its call for papers or information.

On the 22d of May, of the same year, the Senate, on motion of Mr. Benton, requested the President to inform the Senate whether any engagement or agreement had taken place between the President of the United States and the President of Texas in relation to naval or military aid or any other aid, and, if so, to communicate all the particulars and copies of the same, if in writing, and a copy of all communications on the subject; which information was furnished.

On the 28th of May, of the same year, a similar resolution was passed, calling for a copy of the instructions given in 1829 by President Jackson, through the Secretary of State, to the United States minister at Mexico on the subject of Texas; which was furnished.

On the same 28th of May, 1844, on motion by Mr. Benton, the Senate called on the President for "the whole of the private letter from London, with its date, quoted by the American Secretary of State" in a letter of his to the United States chargé d'affaires in Texas, together with the name of the writer of the private letter; which information was supplied without protest.

Numerous other instances occurred about the same time of similar requests and similar compliances, too numerous, indeed, to justify insertion in this report.

The fact that the executive journals of the Senate have only been made public and printed down to the year 1828, and that the written journals since that time are not indexed, makes it difficult to find all the instances of calls on the President and heads of Departments for information and papers that have occurred since that date, but the committee feels safe in stating from the research it has made that the course of the Government has been constant and continuous and unchanged from the beginning until now, and that, in its belief, no instance within the principles and limitations before stated has occurred in which calls for official papers and files addressed either to the President in the form of requests or to the heads of Departments in the form of commands which have not been complied with, but it has sometimes happened where the request to the President was merely a conditional one, leaving it to his discretion whether the papers should be communicated or not, that they have not been communicated.

On the 6th December, 1866, when there was much irritation existing between the houses of Congress and the Executive, the houses of Representatives adopted a resolution directing the Postmaster General to communicate to the House information of all the postmasters removed from office between the 28th July, 1866, and said 6th of December, together with the reasons or causes of such removals, and the names of all persons appointed in their places, &c. This command was, on the 18th February, 1867, complied with by the Postmaster-General without, in the least degree, questioning the right of the House of Representatives to have that information.

Two instances occurring during the administration of President Hayes, under circumstances when there would be naturally a disposition on the part of the Executive to stand upon his constitutional rights, may be of interest. On the 9th January, 1879, the Senate passed a resolution directing the Secretary of the Treasury to transmit charges on file against the Supervising Inspector-General of Steamboats and the papers connected therewith; which was also promptly complied with.

At the same session a similar resolution called for papers on file in the Treasury Department "showing why Lieutenant Devereux was removed from the Revenue Marine Service," which was also complied with.

But it would seem to be needless to array further precedents out of the vast mass that exists in the journals of both houses covering probably every year of the existence of the Government. The practical construction of the Constitution in these respects by all branches of the Government for so long a period would seem upon acknowledged principles to settle what are the rights and powers of the two houses of Congress in the exercise of their respective duties covering every branch of the operations of the Government; and it is submitted with confidence that such rights and powers are indispensable to the discharge of their duties, and do not infringe any right of the Executive, and that it does not belong to either heads of Departments or to the President himself to take into consideration any supposed motives or purposes that either house may have in calling for such papers, or whether their possession or knowledge of their contents could be applied by either house to useful purposes.

The Constitution of the United States was adopted in the light of the well-known history that even ministers of the English Crown were bound to lay before Parliament all papers when demanded, on pain of the instant dismissal of such ministers on refusal, through the rapid and effectual instrumentality of a vote of a want of confidence. And the Continental Congress had for more than ten years itself governed the country and had control of all papers and records, not by reason of anything expressed in the Articles of the Confederation, but by reason of the intrinsic nature of free government. The jurisdiction of the two houses of Congress to legislate, and the power to advise or withhold advice concerning treaties and appointments, necessarily involves the jurisdiction to officially know every step and action of the officers of the law and all the facts touching their conduct in the possession of any Department or even in the possession of the President himself. There was no need to express such a power, for it was necessarily an inherent incident to the exercise of the powers granted.

It will be observed that, in this instance, the call for papers covered a period of more than six months, during which the regular incumbent of the office had been discharging its duties, and also the further period of more than six months, during which the person designated to discharge those duties on suspension of the officer had been acting, and that that person is the one now proposed to be appointed to the place.

It will also be observed that the President has not undertaken to remove the incumbent of the office, but has only, in expressed and stated pursuance of the statutes on the subject, suspended that officer, and that the same statutes expressly provide that such officer shall not be removed without the advice and consent of the Senate, and that, if that advice and consent be not given, the incumbent would (unless his regular term of office should have previously expired) at the close of this session of the Senate, be restored to the lawful right to exercise its duties. The Senate, then, by this nomination, is asked to advise and consent to the removal of the incumbent and to the appointment of the candidate proposed for his place. In exercising its duty in respect of these questions it is plain that the conduct and management of the incumbent is a matter absolutely essential to be known to the Senate in order that it may determine whether it can rightly advise his removal, or rightly leave him to resume the functions of his office at the end of its session, as well as whether the candidate proposed has, in the exercise of the office under his designation, so conducted himself as to show that he is competent and faithful. Indeed, it may be stated with entire accuracy, that even in the case of a vacancy in an office and the proposed filling of such vacancy, it is important for the Senate to know the previous condition and management of the office, the state of its affairs, and whether there have been cases of misconduct or abuse of powers, the embezzlement of money, and, indeed, all the circumstances bearing upon its administration, in order that it may judge of the suitableness of appointing a particular person to take up its duties with reference to the difficulties that may exist in its affairs, the state of its accounts, and everything concerning its administration, so as to measure the fitness and competency of the particular candidate to meet the emergencies of the case.

It appears from the table herewith submitted (Appendix A) that out of about fourteen hundred and eighty-five nominations sent to the Senate during the first thirty days of this session, that is, from the first Monday in December, 1885, to the 5th of January, 1886, six hundred and forty-three were nominations of persons proposed to be appointed in the place of officers suspended and proposed to be removed (and of whom it is known that some are soldiers), and in respect of whom the action of the Senate in advising and consenting to the proposed appointment would effect a removal, and in respect of whom the failure of the Senate to advise and consent to such removals and appointments the effect would be to restore them to the possession of their offices at the end of the session, except in cases in which the terms of some of them should have previously expired.

Is it not desirable and necessary to the proper performance of its duties, and in every aspect of the public interest, that the simple facts in regard to what the conduct of these officials, as well as in regard to what the conduct of the persons designated to perform their duties has been, should be made known to the Senate? Have these suspended officials, or any considerable number of them, been guilty of misconduct in office, or of any personal conduct making them unworthy to be longer trusted with the performance of duties imposed upon them by law? If they have, it would seem to be clear that every consideration of public interest and of public duty would require that the facts should be made known, in order that the Senate may understandingly and promptly advise their removal, and that the most careful scrutiny should be had in respect of selecting their successors, as well as in respect of providing better means and safeguards by legislation for administering the laws of the United States. Such information, it would seem, the Executive is determined the Senate shall not possess, for the alleged reason that it might enable the Senate to understand what circumstances connected with the faithful execution of the laws induced the President to exercise the discretion the statute confers upon him to suspend them, and ask the Senate to unite with him in their removal from office. A similar result would follow in respect of the knowledge of any and every step in the transactions of the Government; for instance, the President as commander-in-chief of the Army has as large discretion as he has in the suspension of civil officers, but on the theory suggested by the Attorney-General, both the President and the Secretary of War would be justified in refusing to either house of Congress copies of papers and documents relating to the administration of the Department of War, and the disposition of the troops, &c., for the reason that the facts being disclosed, the two houses of Congress might be enabled to comprehend the reasons and motives actuating the Executive in his conduct as commander-in-chief.

Reduced to its simplest form, the proposition would be that neither the President nor the head of a Department is bound to communicate any official papers to either house of Congress which might draw into question in the minds of its members or of the people the wisdom or fairness of his acts. But the committee is of the opinion that in matters of this nature the Senate has little concern with the reasons or motives either of the heads of Departments or of the Executive, but it has large concern that its own reasons and grounds of action should rest upon and be drawn from the solid truth. The Senate, if it does its duty and preserves the independence that belongs to it, must act upon its own reasons and judgment and not upon those of the President, however valuable they may be. If the truth regarding the conduct of these officials and designated persons were known the question for the Senate would be, not what were the reasons or motives of the Executive, but whether the facts themselves, as they took place, would furnish it with sufficient reason for giving or withholding its advice and consent to the proposed changes.

Another view of the matter is not, as the committee thinks, without large importance to the public interest at this time. The President in his last annual message, and in connection with the subject of removing the ordinary administration of the laws and the selection of public agents from the arena of mere party politics, stated:

I am inclined to think that there is no sentiment more general in the minds of the people of our country than a conviction of the correctness of the principle upon which the law enforcing civil-service reform is based. In its present condition the law regulates only a part of the subordinate public positions throughout the country. It applies the test of fitness to applicants for these places by means of a competitive examination, and gives large discretion to the Commissioners as to the character of the examination and many other matters connected with its execution. Thus the rules and regulations adopted by the Commission have much to do with the practical usefulness of the statute and with the results of its application.

The people may well trust the Commission to execute the law with perfect fairness and with as little irritation as is possible. But of course no relaxation of the principle which underlies it, and no weakening of the safeguards which surround it can be expected. Experience in its administration will probably suggest amendment of the methods of its execution, but I venture to hope that we shall never again be remitted to the system which distributes public positions purely as rewards for partisan service. Doubts may well be entertained whether our Government could survive the strain of a continuance of this system, which upon every change of administration inspires an immense army of claimants for office to lay siege to the patronage of Government, engrossing the time of public officers with their importunities, spreading abroad the contagion of their disappointment, and filling the air with the tumult of their discontent.

The allurements of an immense number of offices and places exhibited to the voters of the land, and the promise of their bestowal in recognition of partisan activity, debauch the suffrage and rob political action of its thoughtful and deliberative character. The evil would increase with the multiplication of offices consequent upon our extension, and the mania for office-holding, growing from its indulgence, would pervade our population so generally that patriotic purpose, the support of principle, the desire for the public good, and solicitude for the nation's welfare, would be nearly banished from the activity of our party contests and cause them to degenerate into ignoble, selfish, and disgraceful struggles for the possession of office and public place.

Civil-service reform enforced by law came none too soon to check the progress of demoralization.

One of its effects, not enough regarded, is the freedom it brings to the political action of those conservative and sober men who, in fear of the confusion and risk attending an arbitrary and sudden change in all the public offices with a change of party rule, cast their ballots against such a chance.

Parties seem to be necessary, and will long continue to exist; nor can it be now denied that there are legitimate advantages, not disconnected with office-holding, which follow party supremacy. While partisanship continues bitter and pronounced, and supplies so much of motive to sentiment and action, it is not fair to hold public officials, in charge of important trusts, responsible for the best results in the performance of their duties, and yet insist that they shall rely, in confidential and important places, upon the work of those not only opposed to them in political affiliation, but so steeped in partisan prejudice and rancor that they have no loyalty to their chiefs and no desire for their success. Civil-service reform does not exact this, nor does it require that those in subordinate positions who fail in yielding their best service, or who are incompetent, should be retained simply because they are in place. The whining of a clerk discharged for indolence or incompetency, who, though he gained his place by the worst possible operation of the spoils system, suddenly discovers that he is entitled to protection under the sanction of civil-service reform, represents an idea no less absurd than the clamor of the applicant who claims the vacant position as his compensation for the most questionable party work.

The civil-service law does not prevent the discharge of the indolent or incompetent clerk, but it does prevent supplying his place with the unfit party worker. Thus, in both these phases, is seen benefit to the public service. And the people who desire good government, having secured this statute, will not relinquish its benefits without protest. Nor are they unmindful of the fact that its full advantages can only be gained through the complete good faith of those having its execution in charge. And this they will insist upon.

This highly important and valuable official communication, in the presence of six hundred and forty-three suspensions from office, would seem to lead to the conclusion that this number of the civil officers of the United States selected to be suspended and removed, had been so derelict in the performance of their functions or guilty of such personal misconduct as to put them in the category of unfaithful public servants, deserving dismissal by the President and the Senate and the condemnation of their countrymen. In such a state of things we think that the common sense of justice and fair play that is so much prized, as we believe, by the people of the United States would require that in some way this large body of men should have an opportunity to know the substance of their alleged misdoings in order that they may either admit their guilt, or, denying it, explain their conduct, or show that the accusations against them were selfish and wicked pretexts, and set up for the mere purpose of obtaining their suspension and ultimate dismissal from office in order that others less capable and worthy might at once receive the honors and emoluments of their places. It is known to every Senator that so far as the Senate has had to do, both with removals and appointments, it has for a great number of years been its practice, when any officer or person was before it for removal or appointment against whom any serious accusation has been made which would, if true, influence the action of the Senate in the case, to cause the person concerned to be informed of the substance of the complaint against him and give him an opportunity to defend himself, and it is also known that at this very session a very considerable number of instances of that kind have occurred and are daily occurring. If the Senate is proceeding upon a false principle in such instances, it is high time that its course in these respects should be reversed, and that hereafter it should act upon such accusations without any knowledge other than that derived from the accusers, and to leave the victims of such injustice to console themselves with the reflection that all parties are now engaged in an effort to reform the Government.

Why should the facts as they may appear from the papers on file be suppressed ? Is it because that, being brought to light, it would appear that malice and misrepresentation and perjury are somewhat abundant, or merely that faithful and competent and honorable officers have been suspended and are proposed to be removed, under the advice and consent of the Senate, in order that places may be found for party men because they are party men or are the special objects of party favor ?

How does it happen, in this time of suggested reform and purer methods in Government, that for the first time it is thought important that the historic and administrative facts relating to the official and personal conduct of officers of the United States should be withheld, and that the administration of the Government should proceed with a secrecy and mystery as great as in the days of the Star Chamber ?

The high respect and consideration that the Senate must always have for the executive office would make it reluctant to adopt either theory. But at present the impenetrable veil remains, and as the committee is unable to suggest any other solution of the riddle, it must leave it until this veil is lifted and the operations of the Government shall again be known.

In this state of things the committee feels it to be its clear duty to report for the consideration of the Senate and for adoption the following resolutions, namely:

Resolved, That the foregoing report of the Committee on the Judiciary be agreed to and adopted.

Resolved, That the Senate hereby expresses its condemnation of the refusal of the Attorney-General, under whatever influence, to send to the Senate copies of papers called for by its resolution of the 25th of January, and set forth in the report of the Committee on the Judiciary, as in violation of his official duty and subversive of the fundamental principles of the Government and of a good administration thereof.

Resolved, That it is, under these circumstances, the duty of the Senate to refuse its advice and consent to proposed removals of officers, the documents and papers in reference to the supposed official or personal misconduct of whom are withheld by the Executive or any head of a Department when deemed necessary by the Senate and called for in considering the matter.

Resolved, That the provision of section 1754 of the Revised Statutes declaring—

That persons honorably discharged from the military or naval service by reason of disability resulting from wounds or sickness incurred in the line of duty, shall be preferred for appointments to civil offices, provided they are found to possess the business capacity necessary for the proper discharge of the duties of such office—

ought to be faithfully and fully put in execution, and that to remove, or to propose to remove, any such soldier, whose faithfulness, competency, and character are above reproach, and to give place to another who has not rendered such service, is a violation of the spirit of the law, and of the practical gratitude the people and Government of the United States owe to the defenders of constitutional liberty and the integrity of the Government.

All of which is respectfully submitted.

GEO. F. EDMUNDS.
JOHN J. INGALLS.
S. J. R. McMILLAN.
GEO. F. HOAR.
JAMES F. WILSON.
WM. M. EVARTS.

APPENDIX A.

The following statement will show the number of suspensions by the President of the United States as indicated by the Executive nominations delivered to the Senate during the first thirty days of the present session, being from the first Monday in December, 1885, to January 5, 1886, both dates inclusive.

Whole number of messages received during the time............................ 1,485

The Judiciary:

Chief justices of Territories	3
Associate justices of Territories	7
United States district attorneys	28
United States marshals	24
Total	62

Finance:

Assistant treasurer	1
Superintendent mint	1
Coiner mint	1
Assayers mint	5
Melters and refiners	2
Collectors internal revenue	61
Total	**71**

Director Mint (removed)	1

Commerce:

Collectors of customs	45
Appraisers of merchandise	20
Surveyors of customs	12
Consuls	57
Consuls-general	5
Examiners of drugs, &c	4
Naval officers of customs	3
Supervising inspectors of steam vessels	5
Total	**151**

Public Lands:

Surveyors-general	7
Receivers public money	20
Registers land offices	24
Principal clerk of surveys, General Land Office	1
Total	**52**

Territories:

Governors Territories	2
Secretaries Territories	2
Total	**4**

Indian affairs:

Indian inspectors	3
Indian agents	13
Total	**16**

Post-offices and post-roads:

Postmasters	278

Foreign relations:

Secretaries of legations	3

Pensions—

Pension agents	6

Grand total of suspensions	643
Grand total of removal	1

APPENDIX B.

[House Report No. 945; Twenty-seventh Congress, second session. Removal from office of Henry H. Sylvester. To accompany Senate bill No. 549. July 27, 1842; laid upon the table.]

Mr. GARRETT DAVIS, from the select committee appointed on the subject, made the following report:

The select committee charged by the House to inquire into "the cause, manner, and circumstances of the removal of Henry H. Sylvester, late a clerk in the Pension Office, with power to send for persons and papers, and to report by bill, resolution, or otherwise," have performed the duties assigned to them, and beg leave to report as follows:

Mr. Sylvester having been removed by the Hon. John C. Spencer, Secretary of War, your committee thought it was proper to notify him of their proceedings, and therefore directed its chairman to inform him of the readiness of the committee to receive any communication which he might desire to make to it, to summon and take the testimony of any witnesses he might wish to have examined, and to invite him to attend its meetings. In reply, the honorable Secretary informed the chairman that he did "not desire to make any communication to the committee, or to have any witnesses summoned by it, or to attend its meetings."

The committee then made a request in writing, of the Secretary, to furnish for its use "a copy of the charges preferred against Henry H. Sylvester, also a copy of the order or letter dismissing him from office, and copies of any other papers in the Department touching his removal."

In his response, the Secretary says: "The letter dismissing Mr. Sylvester was made a *public record* of the Department, and I therefore transmit a copy of it herewith agreeably to your request." "There is no other paper of the description specified in your request, or relating to the subject, on the files of this Department, nor is there any in my possession which is not of a confidential character." "The faithful discharge of the duties devolved upon the heads of Departments frequently renders it of essential importance to *preserve*, as confidential, communications made and received as such, and private honor as well as public policy forbids that a pledge thus given should be violated."

This reply of the honorable Secretary evinces somewhat more of interest in this proceeding; and, though he argues his positions with great earnestness, your committee are constrained to protest against them, as unjust, impolitic, and immoral. What are they, but that the secret charges of concealed informers, however false and calumnious in fact, and from whatever selfish, impure, and dishonorable motives made, even after they have effected the nefarious purpose of removing a faithful officer, who, indeed, may be above all exception, officially and personally, are still of so important and sacred a character, that "private honor as well as public policy" forbids that they should be revealed to a committee of the House, raised for the purpose of investigating the cause of the removal of the *particular officer.*

Are we under a despotism, where the best officers of the Government are to be struck down—by, they know not whom, and for they know not what ? And does the honorable Secretary imagine that he is clothed with the authority and executing the functions of a Fouché ? That the House of Representatives, the grand inquest of the nation, invested by the Constitution with the power to impeach every officer of the Government, and consequently to supervise all their official acts, is to be told, by a Secretary, that the causes and information upon which he bases his official conduct are of too much public interest and of too confidential a character to be disclosed to it ? And this, too, when such information may be unmitigated falsehood, and when this official action involves the oppression of a subordinate, and malversation in office. The committee do not doubt the power and the right of Congress, and of the House of Representatives, to rend the veil that covers these transactions in the Executive Departments, to explore their most hidden recesses, and to drag to the light, and hold up to the nation every such case, in all its revolting deformity of untruth, tyranny, and corruption ; but it preferred the position assumed by the Secretary should remain undisturbed, that its enormity might be the more striking when examined in connection with the facts and circumstances attending the removal of Sylvester.

The copy of the letter dismissing Sylvester, as transmitted by the Secretary of War to the committee, is as follows:

WAR DEPARTMENT, *April* 9, 1842.

SIR: From and after the 10th instant your services as a clerk in the office of the Commissioner of Pensions will be dispensed with.

Your obedient,

JOHN C. SPENCER.

Mr. HENRY SYLVESTER.

The committee then proceeded to take the testimony, in writing, of sundry witnesses, which accompanies this report, and the substance of which is that on Wednesday, the 6th of April last, Mr. Spencer summoned Sylvester to appear before him, upon the charge that he had, on the Monday succeeding the confirmation, by the Senate, of the nomination of Powell to the consulship to Rio de Janeiro, in a public company expressed his belief that the gamblers had bribed the Secretary of State to procure the nomination of Powell.

Sylvester denied the truth of this charge, and added that this imputation upon Mr. Webster had been the subject of general remark and conversation in this city. Whereupon Mr. Spencer observed to Sylvester that he had nothing further at present, and if he should have thereafter Sylvester should hear from him again. On the succeeding Saturday Sylvester was informed, by a messenger in the Department, that the Secretary had sent to the Pension Office for him, after office hours the preceding evening. He immediately went to Mr. Spencer's office, and was informed that he was out. Sylvester returned in about two hours, and requested the chief clerk to inform Mr. Spencer that, in obedience to the message sent him, he was in attendance. The chief clerk stepped into the Secretary's room, and after a few minutes returned and informed Sylvester that the Secretary did not wish to see him, and thereupon handed him the letter by which he was dismissed from his place. It is proven hat, on the preceding Sunday morning, Powell's appointment, and the slander against Mr. Webster in connection with it, were the topics of conversation among several persons of whom Sylvester was not one; and early the next morning (Monday), to use the expressive phrase of a witness, "were in the mouth of everybody."

Sylvester having learned that the honorable Daniel Webster had procured his dismissal upon the allegation that he had made or indorsed the calumny against him in relation to the nomination of Powell, and, being informed by a friend that the President had said if he would satisfy Mr. Webster he should be reinstated, or otherwise provided for, wrote a letter to the honorable Mr. Bates, of the Senate, in which he denied ever having made this imputation against Mr. Webster; and averring that, on the contrary, he had several times, and whenever he had conversed upon the subject, defended the Secretary of State against it. He procured written statements from four gentlemen showing that such had been his exculpation of Mr. Webster in conversations with them, severally, the day preceding and the day when he was said to have made the charge; and he procured Mr. Bates to wait on Mr. Webster, and present to him as well those statements as his own letter to Mr. Bates. Mr. Webster declined to read these papers, and expressed his full belief in the truth of the information, which he said he had received that Sylvester had made the charge against him.

The committee have examined Sylvester, and he swears that he never made, nor intended to make, any such imputation against Mr. Webster; but, on the contrary, upon the faith of information which he had obtained, he repeatedly, and whenever he spoke upon the subject, defended him against it, and *all improper* conduct in connection with the nomination of Powell.

William A. Williams proves that on the Sunday morning succeeding the confirmation, by the Senate, of Powell, he and several others were expressing their surprise at the nomination; and some one having remarked that "Mr. Webster knew how it was done," Sylvester denied that Mr. Webster had anything to do with the nomination.

George W. Crump, chief clerk in the Pension Office, John T. Cochran, a clerk in the War Department, and Henry M. Morfit, esq., prove, that early on the next day, (Monday), being the day on which Sylvester was said to have used the language concerning Mr. Webster for which the Secretary at War had arraigned him, in separate conversations with each of them, Sylvester had expressly exonerated and defended Mr. Webster against this charge.

Upon a deliberate consideration of this branch of the testimony, your committee are altogether satisfied that Sylvester was innocent of having made or indorsed the calumny against Mr. Webster. His explicit denial, and the evidence he adduced, and which established reasonably the negative, ought to have satisfied both Mr. Spencer and Mr. Webster that he was guiltless; and his dismissal by the Secretary of War, for this cause, and in the manner of it, was unjust, capricious, and oppressive treatment.

As an officer, Sylvester was experienced and capable, assiduous and faithful; as a man, he was modest, respectful, honorable, and moral; as a political partisan, he was neither noisy, obtrusive, nor intolerant. In all these points he might well be held up as an example to his superiors in place. The testimony by which his high personal and official character is sustained is abundant and most satisfactory. It is given by General Eaton, a former Secretary of War; by General Parker, chief clerk in the War Department; by Colonel Edwards, the Commissioner of the Pension Bureau, and by Crump, Cochran, Rice, and Evans, clerks of the War Department. These men have known Sylvester long and intimately, and, at the peril of their places, in their testimony, they do him justice, though some of them seemed to feel that, for this cause, they too might be victimized. They all know full well that the most perfect knowledge and attentive performance of the duties of their offices, the greatest fidelity to the Government and the country, the most respectful deportment to their superiors, and the utmost rectitude of conduct and character, when connected with any degree of independence of political sentiment, however quietly and unobtrusively maintained, give no assurance of continuance in place. Your committee know no portion of the American population which is more oppressed and enslaved in will and spirit than the subordinates in the Executive Departments; none among whom there is more mental suffering, arising from a constant dread of being visited with the petty proscription of some small tyrant, "clothed with a little brief authority," by which they and their families are to be deprived of their support. It was the duty of Mr. Spencer, and would have been his pride, had he been animated by sentiments of justice and magnanimity, to have protected such a subordinate as Sylvester.

It would seem quite improbable that the avowed cause, denied and refuted as it was, upon which the two Secretaries professed to act, could have rendered the ire of

Mr. Webster against Sylvester so implacable. He attributes the deep resentment of the Secretary of State to these transactions. The brother-in-law of Sylvester (th Hon. Mr. Hubbard, of New Hampshire) became the security of Mr. Webster, some few years since, to one of the banks in this city for upwards of $3,000, and during the las summer, with a view to meet a part of the debt, Mr. Hubbard drew upon Mr. Webste for a sum of money in favor of Sylvester, and requested him to collect and apply i according to instructions. Sylvester undertook this commission for his kinsman, and by note, advised Mr. Webster that he held such a draft.

In reply, the honorable Secretary of State requested to see Sylvester upon this sul ject at his office. The latter attended accordingly, and yet a second and a third time before he could obtain an interview. Mr. Webster then evinced his displeasure b discourteous and uncivil conduct, neither responding to the ordinary salutation o the part of Sylvester nor asking him to take a seat. Some time afterwards Mr. Hub bard inclosed Sylvester another draft for a small amount on Mr. Webster, and impor tuned him to collect it. Declining to expose himself again to such treatment as h had previously received from Mr. Webster, Sylvester indorsed it and inclosed it in note to him, with a request of payment, but never heard afterwards of the draft o the money. Sylvester communicated these facts to Mr. Hubbard, and, in December last, he was directed by him to hand Mr. Webster's note over to Mr. Morfit, an attor ney, for collection, with a proposition that, if Mr. Webster would pay $1,000 the re mainder might run for a specified time; otherwise suit to be brought upon it. A arrangement was at length adjusted by which Mr. Webster was to pay $1,000 on th 1st of January last, at the Commercial Bank of Boston, and he accordingly drew fo that amount in favor of Hubbard; but he neither had nor placed any funds in ban to meet his paper, and, at maturity, it was dishonored. Sylvester says that he spok freely of these matters, and of this, he doubts not, Mr. Webster was informed.

But whatever other reasons may have operated in the removal of Sylvester, it is no to be doubted that the ordinary one of making a place for a political friend and par tisan had its full force. His successor is Mr. F. H. Davidge, whose name had bee before the President for an appointment since the 4th of March, 1841. John B. Jones editor of the Madisonian, proves that Mr. Davidge had been writing for his paper, an that some of his contributions were on hand when he received this appointment, an were afterwards inserted; but that the President then requested him to dispense wit the further services of Mr. Davidge as a writer for the Madisonian, which he did Here is the mode by which office seekers qualify themselves for places under this ad ministration. They come to this city and have their names thrown before the Presi dent for an appointment; they commence writing for the Madisonian, under his sur veillance, and, after having gone through the probation, and established their fitnes for *office* by inditing stupid panegyrics upon the President and coarse ribaldry upon the majority in Congress, to be published in the *court journal*, are duly installed int place. Is such the purpose for which the offices of this Government were created and such the principle upon which they are to be filled? What becomes of the mes sage of the President, and of his proclamation, through the Secretary of State, agains the interference of all office holders in politics? Where is the potency of his emphati quotation to them, forbidding active partisanship, "thus far thou comest, but n farther!" Mr. Davidge entered a novice into the Pension Bureau, and merely per forms a portion of the duties which had been previously done by another clerk, Evans and the only result of his labors is to relieve Evans of an occasional press of business yet he receives a salary of $1,400 and Evans but $1,200 It appears, also, that a son of Mr. Davidge has received a clerkship in one of the Departments.

Mr. Madison, in his speech in the House of Representatives in 1789, on the powe of removal from office by the President, says: "The danger, then, consists merely i this—the President can displace from office a man whose merits require that he shoul be continued. What will be the motives which the President can feel for such abus of his power, and the restraints to prevent it? In the first place, he will be impeach able by this House, before the Senate, for such an act of malversation; for I conten that the wanton removal of meritorious officers would subject him to impeachmen and removal from his own high place." The committee concur fully in the soundnes of Mr. Madison's opinion of the responsibility of the President for such an abuse o power, and they do not doubt that this principle applies to all officers of Governmen who are invested with the discretion of removing others. They believe that the hon orable John C. Spencer has been guilty of this official malversation in displacin Sylvester, and they would not hesitate to recommend to the House to impeach hin before the Senate, but that he is in some degree excused by similar abuses, which have so often occurred in the administration of the Executive department during th last thirteen years.

But the case of Sylvester is another of the numerous instances, which warns us o the enormity and the danger of suffering the President and his Departments to wield this formidable power unchecked, and without the least effective responsibility. I with hundreds of others of equal atrocity, cries aloud to Congress to interpose a rem edy, as well to prevent a vast mass of individual oppression, as to uphold purity in the administration of the Government and the public liberty. The practice of treating all the offices of this great Government as "the spoils of victory," and, with the rise and fall of contending parties, the ejection of a large multitude of experienced, honest, and capable incumbents, to make room for needy mercenaries, who entered the political conflict without any principle or love of country, but impelled wholly by a hope of plunder, is the greatest and most threatening abuse that has ever invaded our system. It makes the President the *great feudatory* of the nation, and all offices *fiefs*, whose tenure is *suit and service* to him. It is because all those *fiefs* are at his sovereign will, to be confirmed or granted anew after each Presidential election, that the whole country is kept perpetually convulsed by that oft-recurring and all-absorbing event.

Suppose the successful candidate for this high office had as many real estates, diffused over this Union, as there are offices of Government, those estates producing annually a revenue equal to the salary of each office, and he had the power to bestow and reclaim them at pleasure, would not the possession, by the President, of such a vast means of operating upon the will and controlling the actions of an immense number of the people of this country, scattered everywhere over it, fill all with a dread apprehension of the overthrow of our institutions and of popular liberty? The President has all this tremendous power, in fact, and in the much more dangerous form of bestowing public offices, according to the provisions of the Constitution and laws, seemingly for the exclusive good of the people, and to conduct the necessary operations of the Government. The extent to which it is liable, and, in truth, has been abused, some of the most powerful minds which the country has ever produced have delineated with a vigor and vividness that must strongly impress the most careless.

In 1826 Mr. Benton made a report to the Senate, embracing, in part, this subject, which ought to be carefully read by every American. In that paper we find this powerful passage: "The King of England is 'the fountain of honor;' the President of the United States is the source of patronage. He presides over the entire system of Federal appointments, jobs, and contracts. He has power over the 'support' of the individuals who administer the system. He makes and unmakes them. He chooses from the circle of his friends and supporters, and may dismiss them, and, upon all the principles of human actions, he will dismiss them as often as they disappoint his expectations. There may be exceptions, but the truth of the general rule is proved by the exception. The intended check and control of the Senate, without new constitutional or statutory provisions, will cease to operate. Patronage will penetrate this body, subdue its capacity of resistance, chain it to the car of power, and enable the President to rule as easily and much more securely with than without the nominal check of the Senate.

"If the President himself was the officer of the people, elected by them and responsible to them, there would be less danger from this concentration of all power in his hands; but it is the business of statesmen to act upon things as they are, and not as they would wish them to be. We must look forward to the time when the public revenue will be doubled; when the civil and military officers of the Government will be quadrupled; when its influence over individuals will be multiplied to an indefinite extent; when the nomination of the President can carry any man through the Senate, and his recommendation can carry any measure through the two houses of Congress; when the principle of public action will be open and avowed—the President wants my vote, and I want his patronage; I will vote as he wishes, and he will give me the office I wish for. What will this be but the government of one man? And what is the government of one man but a monarchy? Names are nothing. The nature of a thing is in its substance, and the name soon accommodates itself to the substance." "Those who make the President must support him. Their political fate becomes identified, and they must stand or fall together. Right or wrong, they must support him," &c. All this was prophecy then; it is now history.

In the year 1835 Mr. Calhoun took up the subject of Executive patronage generally, and submitted to the Senate a measure for its reduction, accompanied by a most elaborate and able report. Upon this branch of the subject he says:

"It is only within the last four years that removals from office have been introduced as a system; and, for the first time, an opportunity has been afforded of testing the tendency of the practice, and witnessing the mighty increase which it has given to the force of Executive patronage, and the entire and fearful change, in conjunction with other causes, it is effecting in our political system. Nor will it require much reflection to perceive in what manner it contributes to increase so vastly the extent of Executive patronage."

"So long as offices were considered as public trusts, to be conferred on the honest, the faithful, and capable, for the common good, and not for the benefit or gain of the incumbent or his party, and so long as it was the practice of the Government to continue in office those who faithfully performed their duties, its patronage, in point of fact, was limited to the mere power of nominating to accidental vacancies or to newly

S. Rep. 135——2

created offices, and would, of course, exercise but a moderate influence, either over the body of the community or over the officeholders themselves; but when this practice was reversed—when offices, instead of being considered as public trusts, to be conferred on the deserving, were regarded as the spoils of victory, to be bestowed as rewards for partisan service—it is easy to see that the certain, direct, and inevitable tendency of such a state of things is to convert the entire body of those in office into corrupt and supple instruments of power, and to raise up a host of hungry, greedy, and subservient partisans, ready for every service, however base and corrupt. Were a premium offered for the best means of extending, to the utmost, the power of patronage; to destroy the love of country, and to substitute a spirit of subserviency and man worship; to encourage vice and to discourage virtue; and, in a word, to prepare for the subversion of liberty and the establishment of a despotism, no scheme more perfect could be devised; and such must be the tendency of the practice, with whatever intention adopted, or to whatever extent pursued."

The remedy proposed, both by Mr. Benton and Mr. Calhoun, to reduce this inordinate power, was to pass a law repealing the section of the act of 1820 which limited the appointment of certain officers to four years; and, also, requiring the President, when he removed any officer, to lay the cause of his removal, at the time of nominating his successor, before the Senate.

Mr. Webster supported this measure of Mr. Calhoun's in a speech of unsurpassed ability, in which he said:

"I concur with those who think that, looking to the present, and looking also to the future, and regarding all the probabilities of what is before us, as to the qualities which shall belong to those who may fill the Executive chair, it is important to the stability of Government and the welfare of the people that there should be a check to the progress of official influence and patronage. The unlimited power to grant office, and to take it away, gives a command over the hopes and the fears of a vast multitude of men. It is generally true that he who controls another man's means of living controls his will. Where there are favors to be granted, there are usually enough to solicit for them; and when favors, once granted, may be withdrawn at pleasure, there is ordinarily little security for personal independence of character. The power of giving office thus affects the fears of all who are in and the hopes of all who are out. Those who are out endeavor to distinguish themselves by active political friendship, by warm personal devotion, by clamorous support of men in whose hands is the power of reward; while those who are in, ordinarily take care that others shall not surpass them in such qualities or such conduct as is most likely to secure favor. They resolve not to be outdone in any of the works of partisanship. The consequence of all this is obvious. A competition ensues, not of political labors, not of rough and severe toils for the public good, not of manliness, independence, and public spirit, but of complaisance, of indiscriminate support of Executive measures, of pliant subserviency, and gross adulation. All throng and rush together to the altar of man worship, and there they offer sacrifices and pour out libations till the thick fumes of their incense turn their own heads, and turn also the head of him who is the object of their idolatry.

"Sir, we cannot disregard our own experience. We cannot shut our eyes to what is around us and upon us. No candid man can deny that a great, a very great change has taken place, within a few years, in the practice of the Executive government, which produced a corresponding change in our political condition. No one can deny that office of every kind is now sought with extraordinary avidity, and that the condition, well understood to be attached to every office, high or low, is indiscriminate support of Executive measures, and implicit obedience to Executive will. For these reasons, sir, I am for arresting the further progress of Executive patronage, if we can arrest it. I am for staying the further contagion of this plague."

This extract is fraught with momentous truths, and some of the gravest of them are enforced by the present political position of the intellectual giant who gave them utterance. When he illustrates them, not less by his own lamentable example than by the graphic vigor with which he has stated them, who can refuse to give heed to the solemn lesson which they teach?

Mr. Clay also gave the same measure his earnest support, and, in the course of his argument on the occasion, he said: "We can now deliberately contemplate the vast expansion of Executive power under the present administration, free from embarrassment. And is there any real lover of civil liberty who can behold it without great and just alarm? Take the doctrines of the protest and the Secretary's report together, and, instead of having a balanced Government, with three co-ordinate departments, we have but one power in the state. According to these papers, all officers concerned in the administration of the laws are bound to obey the President. His will controls every branch of the administration. No matter that the laws may have assigned to other officers of the Government specially defined duties; no matter that the theory of the Constitution and the law supposes them bound to the discharge of those duties according to their own judgment, and under their own responsibility, and liable to impeachment for malfeasance; the will of the President, even in opposition to their own deliberate sense of their own obligations, is to prevail, and expulsion from office is to be the penalty of disobedience."

"The basis of this overshadowing superstructure of Executive power is the power of dismission, which it is the object of one of the bills under consideration somewhat to regulate, but which, it is contended by the supporters of the Executive authority, is uncontrollable. The practical exercise of this power, during this administration, has reduced the salutary co-operation of the Senate, as approved by the Constitution, in all appointments, to an idle form. What avail is it that the Senate shall have passed upon a nomination if the President at any time thereafter, even the next day, whether the Senate be in session or vacation, without any known cause, may dismiss the incumbent? Let us examine the nature of this power. It is exercised in the recesses of the Executive mansion, perhaps upon *secret* information. The accused officer is not *present or heard*, nor confronted with the witnesses against him, and the President is judge, juror, and executioner. *No reasons* are assigned for the dismission, and the public is left to conjecture the cause. Is not a power so exercised essentially a despotic power? It is adverse to the genius of all free government, the foundation of which is responsibility. Responsibility is the vital principle of civil liberty, as irresponsibility is the vital principle of despotism. Free government can no more exist without this principle than animal life can be sustained without the presence of the atmosphere. But is not the President absolutely irresponsible in the exercise of this power? How can he be reached? By impeachment? It is a mockery."

How is this corrupting and tremendous power to be bridled? All the great men who advocated the measure of Mr. Benton and Mr. Calhoun, whilst they maintained it would effect much good, conceded it would be a very inadequate remedy. In the opinion of your committee, a more effective one would be for Congress to pass a law repealing the limitation to office under the law of 1820, and requiring all officers having the power to dismiss a subordinate to furnish each person removed from office with the cause, in writing; and also to report forthwith the name of the officer, and the cause of his removal to the President; and that the President, at the ensuing session of Congress, report to each House a full list of all officers removed since the preceding session, with the cause, severally, of their removal; and, also, that the Senate assert and maintain its constitutional right to concur or to refuse to concur in the removal of every officer to whose nomination it has advised and consented. As to the first branch of this proposition, there can be no doubt of the power of Congress to establish it by law. The second section of the second article of the Constitution provides: "But the Congress may by law vest the appointment of such inferior officers as they think proper in the President, in the courts of law, or in the heads of Departments."

If Congress were to pass, as it has passed, many such laws, thus vesting the appointment of inferior officers, it could prescribe a particular mode for their removal, and any other conditions that might be thought proper. The justice and sound policy of *that condition* is undeniable. All offices are created exclusively for the convenience and benefit of the people; and, whilst none belong to the incumbent, certainly none belong to the incumbent of *any other office*. No removal should ever take place except when the *public weal* requires it; and whenever and wherever such is the state of the fact, there is a specific cause why it is so. If there be no such cause, no removal ought to be made, as, independent of its generally dangerous and corrupting tendency, it might be both unjust to the individual officer and detrimental to the public service. There might be no cause, and yet one might be falsely assumed; wherefore, the officer exercising this power ought to be required to set forth to the person dismissed the ground of the proceeding, that he, knowing its truth or its falsehood, might have an opportunity to arraign his superior for an abuse of power, both before the country and Congress. All such cases ought to be reported to Congress, that it might know how a power which it had authorized was executed, and that it might correct and punish its perversion.

Why should there be any secrecy in these matters? Secrecy is not an element of our system—its great and fundamental law is public opinion; and how can this be wisely and justly formed when the facts which are necessary to enlighten it are concealed as "*state secrets?*" It is only falsehood and corruption, wrong and oppression, that are sought to be wrapped in darkness; the officer who means and acts well dreads not the sunlight. There may be rare cases, where secrecy in the removal of public officers would promote the public good; but the mischief and immorality inseparable from such a system will preponderate a thousand fold.

The clause repealing the section of the act of 1820 which limits the appointment of certain officers to four years, it is also believed, will be of great practical utility. All those officers at the termination of that period are, by operation of law, removed for the President, without any act on his part; and he may commit the greatest improprieties in filling the vacant places without incurring any liability for the displacement of faithful public agents. This regulation swells considerably his power, as it makes a great many vacancies with the certainty of the returning year, and subjects the incumbents more inexorably to his will than if the exertion of the power of removal were a preliminary operation. Such repeal would, besides, add somewhat to the permanency and certainty of the tenure by which office would be held; and such tenure should at least be as certain and permanent as the fidelity and fitness of the officer.

But warped from some of its most essential and fundamental principles, as our Government has been, by the vast accession to the power of the Executive, the only mode by which it can be demonarchized is to return to that great conservative principle of the Constitution, that the President, by his single action, cannot permanently and absolutely displace any officer. He is made the depository of the *executive power, and the whole executive power of our Government*—not an indigested and vague executive power—not that of France, or of England, of Russia, or of Turkey, of this age, or of any past one, but as it is defined, established, organized, and circumscribed by our own Constitution; and he cannot, without usurpation, wield one particle more. Our fathers conceived and fabricated their own edifice of Government; they mixed and compounded different principles, but they made the structure complete after its own order. The ideas attached to the phrases "legislative powers," "executive power," and "judicial power," as used in our Constitution, are unique, and their significance is only to be learned correctly as they are taught in that instrument.

There are certain powers of our Government that are purely *legislative* others purely *executive* and others purely *judicial;* and there are certain other powers that belong to *neither* of those classes; and because they are to be exercised by one of the departments, or a branch thereof, does not make them legislative, executive, or judicial. The House of Representatives may impeach officers of the Government; and, when the electors fail to elect the President, is to choose that officer, and yet neither of these acts is of a legislative character. The President, by and with the advice and consent of the Senate, is clothed with the full appointing power. The function of the Senate to approve or reject the President's nominations is not legislative; nor is it executive in our system, because, to be so, it must appertain to the *President*. Neither is the act of nominating to office an executive power. or indeed, of *itself, any power;* it is merely a constituent, an element of a power, to be furnished by the agency of the President, as the other constituent is to be produced by the action of the Senate. If the President's nomination be rejected, nothing has been effected by it; both must concur and combine to constitute a power, a faculty in the business of the Government.

From these plain principles it is apparent that theoretical constructions of the provisions and powers of our Constitution, by analogies drawn from other Governments, are very liable, as they have led to great errors; and, as a general rule, it is much safer to construe our Constitution of itself, and by itself, especially as it is a Government, not of original and plenary, but of delegated and limited, powers. Though the power of appointment, in our peculiar system, is given conjointly to the President and the Senate, yet their action is separate and independent, and each equally necessary to effect the result. The "advice and consent" of the Senate is as indispensable as the nomination of the President to fill an office.

The Constitution is wholly silent upon the subject of removals from office, except by impeachment; and if another and more summary mode of displacing a faithless or incompetent officer is necessary and proper to secure a due execution of the laws, the position might be very plausibly assumed that *the mode* would involve an implied legislative power, and was therefore vested in Congress. This position would be strongly supported by quoting from the Constitution: "Congress shall have power to make all laws which shall be necessary and proper for carrying into execution the foregoing powers, and all other powers vested by this Constitution in the *Government* of the United States, or in *any department* or *office* thereof." But the more general opinion seems to be that the power of appointment implies and carries along with it the power of removal. That *a* power to create imports *the* power to destroy may be assumed to be a general truth, both in logic and philosophy; and this principle would lead directly to the conclusion that the power of appointment and removal are blended, but for the clause in the Constitution before quoted. However, the committee will not further controvert the general judgment on this point.

It is believed that there are but few statesmen or jurists in our country but who concede that an officer cannot be constitutionally removed by the President without the concurrence of the Senate, and that practice and pretty general acquiescence alone sanction the contrary doctrine. In the case of Hennen *ex parte,* the Supreme Court have decided that Congress had authorized the United States district courts to appoint their clerks, and, "in the absence of all *constitutional provision or statutory regulation,* it would seem to be a sound and *necessary* rule to consider the power of removal as incident of the power of appointment." The judgment of the court, consequently, was, that the district court could, at pleasure, remove its clerk. Here is a recognition of the general principle, by the highest judicial tribunal of the nation;

and it is strictly applicable to the question now under examination, because there is no clause in the Constitution, except that which establishes and regulates the power of appointment, from whence a power of removal, in any mode except by impeachment, can be deduced.

In the execution of this auxiliary power of removal, it would be just as logical for the Senate to contend for an exclusive right to remove from office as that the President should; for either to do so would be equally paradoxical. The power which is implied and incidental must be congruous with the express and the principal power; and it is absurd to say that though both the President and the Senate must combine, by distinct and independent operation, to effect a certain act, yet that *he*, in the exercise of a faculty only inferred from what he *is expressly* authorized to do, may, the next hour and at all times afterwards, reverse and abrogate the joint act of himself and the Senate. The political effect would be yet more preposterous. The Senate is expressly established by the Constitution as a check upon the President in the execution of the appointing power. If the power of removal be accorded to him absolutely and exclusively, it practically destroys this restraint, and the power *expressly* conferred upon the Senate becomes to be expunged by the *implied* power of the President. Whenever an officer refused to submit to his will, and to carry out his culpable objects, or, from any cause, was obnoxious to him, he would immolate him by his own stern fiat; and the utmost the Senate could do would be to force him to nominate a succession of his favorites and tools. The framers of the Constitution did not do their work after this manner.

The connection between the President and the Senate, in the appointing power, continues in all its forms, whether express or incidental. So, if the Constitution had required the approval of the House of Representatives also, of the President's nominations to office, the power of removal would have been incidental to the President and the two houses of Congress, and all would necessarily have to concur to dismiss an officer. The implied power is to the principal and express one what the shade is to the substance ; when the latter exists in a duplicate form, the former cannot be single, but is stamped with and represents the perfect figure of the thing which gives it existence. We are examining what the Constitution is, not what it ought to be; and yet, with the construction which we give it, we are prepared to maintain that it is exactly what it should be.

It was during the first session of the first Congress under our Constitution that a legislative construction was given to that instrument, which vested the power of removal in the President alone. Such members of the convention as were then in Congress were equally divided on this (then new) question. Washington was the man to whom the power was to be accorded or denied. The Senate was equally divided, and its decision was rendered by the casting vote of the *Vice-President;* whilst the majority in the House was not large. The pure minds of those who maintained the position that this was an Executive power, and belonged to the President exclusively, could not conceive the flagitious abuse that has since marked its exercise ; and if, after all the impressive admonition of subsequent experience, the men who established that unfortunate heresy could be recalled from the tomb to consider the question now for the first time, it is impossible to doubt that they would settle it differently.

The considerations then urged in support of the position, that this power was appendant to the President alone, are mainly those of *convenience, expediency, necessity:* and the strength of the argument, embracing constitutional law, the sound sense of the case, and a safe policy, are clearly on the other side of the question. Under every Administration, previous to 1829, except that of Mr. Jefferson, it was a dormant power ; as no other President, in eight years, exceeded twelve removals, and all were for cause which the Senate would probably have deemed sufficient, and which were therefore silently ratified by the country. Even Mr. Jefferson removed but about forty officers in his two terms; and the reason why the people did not manifest a greater repugnance to his exercise of this power was, that much the larger number of the offices of Government were held by his political opponents.

In 1829, a wary and keen-sighted party thought it could descry that this power was about to be exerted by the existing Administration for the proscription of political opinions; and then its constitutional authority was boldly and justly denied. This construction was given in a speculative form in 1789; it was never practically asserted until 1801, and only for a brief season and to a very limited extent. So soon as it was deliberately examined by the generation of men who succeeded those by whom it was originally made, upon the presumption that it was about to become an active administrative power, the weight of the highest reason and of the most erudite attainments of the whole country decided against it. That decision is still unreversed and in full force ; so that this anomalous and unconstitutional power has not the sanction of general acquiescence to sustain it.

Your committee concede, that where the constitutionality of a power is doubtful, and yet it is *highly expedient and proper* that it should exist, and it has been exerted by successive Congresses, approved and confirmed by the other departments of the Government, and ratified and sustained the by people, all this concurring must be considered as conclusive of the question. But where a power, like the one now controverted, has only been prospectively considered and recognized, and long before any case for its exercise had arisen, the weight of authority for and against it being, then, nearly an equipoise, the power itself not being necessary for a due administration of the Government, but tending irresistibly to its corruption, the destruction of its checks and balances, and the overthrow of popular liberty, your committee are far from thinking that it is entitled to the consideration due such a sanction; on the contrary, they have no hesitation in recommending its unconditional and immediate renunciation.

They will now proceed to fortify their general position of hostility to this power, by the weight of some of the greatest men which our country has ever produced. Mr. Benton, in his report before quoted from, says: "It is no longer true that the President, in dealing out offices to members of Congress, will be limited, as supposed in the Federalist, to the inconsiderable number of places which may become vacant by the ordinary casualties of death and resignations; on the contrary, he may now draw, for that purpose, upon the whole entire fund of the Executive patronage. Construction and legislation have effected this change.

"In the first year of the Constitution, a construction was put upon that instrument, which enabled the President to create as many vacancies as he pleased, and at any moment he thought proper. This was effected by yielding to him the *kingly prerogative* of dismissing officers without the formality of trial. The authors of the Federalist had not foreseen this construction; so far from it, they had asserted the contrary, and, arguing logically from the premises, 'that the dismissing power was appertinent to the appointing power,' they had maintained, in No. 77 of that standard work, that, as the consent of the Senate was necessary to the appointment, so the consent of the same body would be equally necessary to his dismission from office. But this construction was overruled by the first Congress which was formed under the Constitution; the power of dismission from office was *abandoned* to the President alone; and, with the *acquisition* of this prerogative alone, the *power* and patronage of the Presidential office was instantly increased to an indefinite extent," &c.

Mr. Webster's speech in favor of the bill reported by Mr. Calhoun is among the most cogent and powerful emanations of his mighty mind. In a series of unanswerable arguments, he assaults and overthrows this exclusive power of the President to dismiss from office, and concludes: "On the whole, sir, with the diffidence which becomes one who is reviewing the opinions of some of the ablest and wisest men of the age, I must still express my own conviction that the decision of Congress, in 1789 *which separated* the power of removal from the power of appointment, was founded on an erroneous construction of the Constitution, and that it has led to great inconsistencies as well as to great abuses in the subsequent, and especially in the more recent, history of the Government.

"I think, then, sir, that the power of appointment naturally and necessarily includes the power of removal, where no limitation is expressed, nor any tenure but that at will declared. The power of appointment being conferred on the President and Senate, I think the power of removal went along with it, and should have been regarded as a part of it, and exercised by the same hands. I think, consequently, that the decision of 1789, which implied a power of removal separate from the appointing power, was erroneous.

"But I think the decision of 1789 has been established and recognized by subsequent law as the settled construction of the Constitution, and that it is our duty to act upon the case accordingly, for the *present*, without *admitting* that Congress may not, if necessity shall require it, *reverse* the decision of 1789. I think the legislature possesses the power of *regulating the condition, duration, qualification*, and *tenure of offices* in all cases where the Constitution has made *no express provision* upon the subject."

Mr. Clay also controverts this noxious interpolation of the Constitution with extraordinary force of argument, and, after having made a luminous analysis of the precedent by which it was established, he denies that it is conclusive, and adds: "A precedent established against the weight of argument, by a House of Representatives greatly divided, in a Senate equally divided, under the influence of a reverential attachment to the Father of his Country, upon the condition that, if the power were applied, as we know it has been in hundreds of instances recently applied the President himself would be justly liable to impeachment and removal from office; and which, until this administration, has never, since its adoption, been thoroughly examined or considered." Mr. Clay gave Mr. Calhoun's bill his hearty support, and he prepared an amendment and gave notice of his intention to offer it which provided, in substance, that the President should exercise the power of removal only in concurrence with the Senate; when the Senate was not in session he might suspend an officer, but was required to communicate the fact, together with the cause to the Senate, at its next session; and unless that body concurred, the suspended officer to be *ipso facto* reinstated in his place.

In the opinion of the committee, this proposition of Mr. Clay comprehends the true exposition of the Constitution. The President is exclusively invested with the appointing power, to fill all vacancies happening during the recess of the Senate, the duration of the appointment being limited by the termination of its ensuing session. If the power of removal is incident to, attendant upon, and correspondent with, the power of appointment, it would follow that the President, during the recess of the Senate, would be authorized to exercise a correlative power of removal. As his appointments, made at such times, would determine and expire at the end of the ensuing session of the Senate, so his removals or suspensions from office would be operative only for the same period; and, unless the Senate also agreed to the dismissal of the officer, he would, by operation of the constitutional principle, be fully reinstated in his place. Whilst the Senate was in session the President could not displace any more than he could appoint an officer, but would have to state his decision to remove, together with the cause, to the Senate; and unless it advised and consented thereto no removal would ensue.

This construction, it is believed, is in strict conformity both to the letter and the spirit of the Constitution, and would bring back the administration of the Government to its true principles. It would tend greatly to reduce the collossal power of the President and to restore to the other departments their just constitutional weight and independence. It would not impair the necessary energy and efficiency of the Executive branch, or obstruct in any considerable degree the proper responsibility to which inferior officers ought to be held. For faithlessness, incompetency, or any other cause the President could suspend, and the reasonable presumption is that whenever it was right that the officer should be permanently displaced the Senate would ratify his act. Some inconvenience would no doubt be produced by this practice—a bad officer might be occasionally continued in place longer than would be compatible with the public interest—the Senate might have more business thrown upon it; but with all its inconveniencies, even if the sessions of the Senate were thereby made perpetual, it would be incomparably preferable to existing things. The one would introduce only transient and minor evils, the other is certainly bringing on the subversion of our whole system of constitutional liberty.

But there would be other beneficial consequences of the utmost importance. A great appreciation in the character of our public officers, particularly in the inferior grades, would ensue. From the degradation of physical and moral servitude, they would rise to the dignity of free and independent thought, opinion, and action; they would exchange the trembling uncertainty of a ceaseless dread of the oppression of bad men for a reasonable assurance that qualifications, fidelity, and decorum in office would enable them to maintain their places. The President and the Senate would become, what the Constitution intended they should be, mutual checks; and both would then be subject to a proper responsibility at the bar of public opinion, and be required to justify every case of removal. This would be a valuable immunity to inferior officers.

When this reform should have had time to operate, and to produce its legitimate fruits, there would not be a great many cases in which it would be necessary to exercise the power of removal. The subordinate being no longer subject to the tyrant's law—the uncontrolled will of one man—he would begin to feel too much security, and cherish too much self-respect, to play the parasite and the pander. Rising with the consciousness that he now belonged to the country, and not to his official superior, patriotism and a sense of duty would take the place of supple hypocrisy and venal man worship. Occupying a position to mark official malfeasance, both above and below him, each officer would be a sentinel on his associates, because he would know that he would be rewarded, and not dismissed and punished, for the revelation of their delinquencies. Officers exercising the power of appointing to inferior places, not being able to reduce their nominees to the condition of minions, would at length begin to feel the promptings of a sense of duty and a regard for their own fame, and look for moral and business qualities.

The infamous spoils system, with all its abhorrent and demoralizing concomitants, would be overthrown. The Presidential election—that moral volcano which breaks forth periodically in its terrible eruptions, and in the intervals keeps the whole country heaving and tossing in wild commotion—would be tamed of that excited and convulsive energy which menaces the overthrow of social order, for it is this power of removal, enabling the President at will to reclaim and regrant fifty thousand places, and thus to sway the hopes and the fears of at least four times that number of men, diffused over the whole Confederacy, which has rendered the Presidential election not the most sober, well-considered, and well-purposed act which this great people perform, but one general and wild conflict of passion, venality, corruption, and violence.

The past assures us of what would be the future state of things, if the principle, that an officer is only to be removed for sufficient cause, should be again established. Under Washington, Madison, Monroe, and the two Adamses it fully obtained, and there was hardly occasion to exert it once the average during each year of the administration of these Presidents, and yet, in those better days of the Republic, the superiority of the officers of the Government over those of this day, in capability, fidelity, and virtue is most striking. The people were then neither better, nor wiser, nor more patriotic, nor more devoted to business than now; nor was our general condition and circumstances more favorable to the preservation of public and private virtue in Government agents. It is the degenerate and demoralizing "spoils principle" which has contributed, more than any other cause, to defile our whole system, and is precipitating us so rapidly upon premature decay and ruin; and we must expel it if we would save our free and glorious institutions.

The present predicament of the Executive power affords no argument against the truth of the positions we have assumed. The President came fortuitously into office, without a party, and not himself occupying the position of a party leader. Repudiating both the party which had elevated him to the Vice-Presidency, and that which had opposed his election, he attempted the irrational and impossible task of building up for himself a third one. This was an impossibility, because the two antagonist parties constituted the entire people, their cohesion having been established by years of affiliation upon distinct and well-contested systems of measures; and because the President himself is very far from being a man who, under the most favorable circumstances, could gather together and form a party. The gigantic Executive power of the Government is, at this time, as near an abstraction, an ideality, notwithstanding the ill-concerted and desperate attempts to make it practically effective, as it is possible to be; but its very repose and inertion will cause it, when aroused and directed by a capable man, to act with renovated vigor. The present conjuncture is most propitious for its reduction. The relaxation of party prejudice and intolerance in a very sensible degree, a calmer and more impartial view of principles, measures, and men, and the total inability of the present incumbent to interpose any obstacle, except by the exercise of the veto, all seem to allure Congress now to attempt this great reform.

Mr. Tyler was a member of the Senate when Mr. Calhoun introduced his measure, and his name is found among the majority of that body which voted for it. His public position has been distinctly that of an advocate of the diminution of Executive power. In his address to the people of the United States, on entering upon the discharge of the duties of the Presidential office, we find the following passage: "In view of the fact, well avouched by history, that the tendency of all human institutions is to concentrate power in the hands of a single man, and that their ultimate downfall has proceeded from this cause, I deem it of the most essential importance that a complete separation should take place between the sword and the purse. No matter how or where the public moneys shall be deposited, so long as the President can exert the power of appointing and removing at his pleasure the agents selected for their custody, the commander-in-chief of the Army and Navy is, in fact, the treasurer. A permanent and radical change should therefore be decreed.

"The patronage incident to the Presidential office, already great, is constantly increasing. Such increase is destined to keep pace with our population, until, without a figure of speech, an army of office holders will overspread the land. The unrestrained power exerted by a selfish, ambitious man, in order either to perpetuate his authority or to hand it over to some favorite as his successor, may lead to the employment of all the means within his control to accomplish his object. The right to remove from office, while subject to no just restraint, is inevitably destined to produce a spirit of crawling servility with the official corps, which, in order to uphold the hands which feed them, would lead to direct and active interference in elections, both State and Federal, thereby subjecting the course of State legislation to the dictation of the chief executive officer, and making the will of that officer absolute and supreme I *will*, at a proper time, invoke the action of Congress upon this subject, and shall readily acquiesce in the adoption of all proper measures which are calculated to arrest these evils, so full of danger in their tendency. I will remove *no incumbent* from office who has faithfully and honestly acquitted himself of the duties of his office, except in such cases where such officers have been guilty of an active partisanship, or by secret means, the less manly, and therefore the more objectionable, has given his official influence to the purposes of party, thereby bringing the patronage of the Government into conflict with the freedom of elections."

In his message to Congress at the commencement of the extra session he again takes up the same subject and treats it thus: "The power of appointing to office is one of a character most delicate and responsible. The appointing power is ever more exposed to be led into error. With anxious solicitude to select the most trustworthy for official station, I cannot be supposed to possess a personal knowledge of the qualifications of every applicant. I deem it therefore proper, in this most public manner, to invite, on the part of the Senate, a just scrutiny into the character and pretensions of every person whom I may bring to their notice in the regular form of a nomination for office. Unless persons every way trustworthy are employed in the public service, corruption and irregularity will inevitably follow. I shall, with the *greatest cheerfulness*, acquiesce in the decision of that body, and, regarding it as wisely constituted to aid the executive department in the performance of this delicate duty, I shall look to its 'consent and advice' as *given only* in furtherance of the best interests of the country. I shall also, at the earliest proper occasion, *invite* the attention of Congress to such measures as, in my judgment, will be best calculated to *regulate and control* the Executive power in reference to this vitally interesting subject."

In his message at the beginning of the present session he again presents this subject, thus: "I feel it my duty to bring under your consideration a practice which has *grown up* in the administration of the Government, and which I am deeply convinced ought to be corrected. I allude to the exercise of power which *usage rather than reason* has vested in the President, of removing incumbents from office, in order to substitute others more in favor with the dominant party. My own conduct in this respect has been governed by a conscientious purpose to exercise the removing power only in cases of unfaithfulness or inability, or in those in which its exercise appeared necessary in order to *discontinue* and *suppress* that spirit of active partisanship, on the part of holders of office, which not only withdraws them from the steady and impartial discharge of their official duties, but exerts an undue and injurious influence over elections, and degrades the character of the Government, inasmuch as it exhibits the Chief Magistrate as being a party, through his agents, in the secret plots or open workings of political parties.

"In respect to the exercise of this power, nothing should be left to discretion which may safely be regulated by law; and it is of high importance to restrain. as far as possible, the stimulus of personal interest in public elections. Considering the great increase which has been made in public offices in the last quarter of a century, and the probability of further increase, we incur the hazard of witnessing violent contests, directed too often to the single object of retaining office by those who are in or obtaining it by those who are out. Under the influence of these convictions, I shall cordially concur in any constitutional measure for regulating, and, by *regulating, restraining* the power of removal." These are just and sensible views, mixed up with a profusion of fine promises, and the country may hope for something from Mr. Tyler when he proceeds to redeem these promises.

In conformity to the opinions herein set forth, your committee ask leave to report the subjoined resolutions, and a bill providing for the repeal of the limitation of four years to the appointment of certain officers, by the act of Congress of 1820; and that, whenever an officer is dismissed, he shall be furnished, by the authority dismissing him, with the cause thereof, in writing; and in every case where the dismission may be made by any other officer or officers than the President, it shall be his or their duty forthwith to report to the President the name of the officer so removed, together with the cause of the removal; and the President to report to both houses of Congress, at its next session, all such cases, with the cause of the removal of each officer.

Resolved, That the Hon. John C. Spencer, Secretary of War, in having removed Henry H. Sylvester, late a clerk in the Pension Office, is properly chargeable with injustice and oppression towards the said Henry H. Sylvester, and of culpable abuse of his authority as Secretary of War.

Resolved. That both houses of Congress, and especially the House of Representatives, as the grand inquest of the nation, have a constitutional right at all times to free access to the Executive Departments of the Government for the examination of all papers therein, whether regarded by the head of the Department as public or as private and confidential; and, also, copies of all such papers, from the officer or officers having their custody, as either house may require.

Resolved, That the power of removal from office is not expressly conferred by the Constitution, but that it is incidental to and derivable from the power of appointment, and is consequently to be exercised by such officers and branches of the Government as are invested by the Constitution and laws with the power of appointment; that a power of removal belongs neither to the President nor the Senate exclusively, but to both conjointly, and as incidental to the separate agency of each in appointing to office; that, as the President is clothed by the Constitution, during the recess of the Senate, with the full appointing power to all vacancies occurring during such recess, his appointment to continue until the end of the ensuing session of the Senate, so he may during such recess exercise the incidental and correlative power of removal, to have effect for the same time, and at the next ensuing session of the Senate it is his *constitutional duty* to lay before that body the names of all officers whom he may have removed during its preceding vacation, *together with the cause, specifically, of the removal;* and if the Senate do, at that session, advise and consent to such removal, the said officer is thereupon absolutely and permanently displaced—otherwise he is, by the operation of the Constitution, at the end of said session, reinstated in his office, with all his rights and privileges; and where the President, during the session of the Senate, decides to remove an officer, it is his duty, under the Constitution, to communicate the name of such officer to the Senate, with the specific cause for his removal; and unless that body advise and consent to the removal of such officer, no removal whatever takes place, and he continues in his office, as though there had been no such proceeding against him.

The undersigned, a member of the committee appointed on the case of Henry H. Sylvester, concurs in the report of the majority of said committee, so far as it is a statement of the facts and circumstances attending the removal of said Sylvester; and he also concurs in the first resolution submitted by the majority. But, although he finds much to approve in the residue of the report of the majority, and with pleasure bears his testimony to the great force and ability with which it is drawn, he dissents from it in the main, and also from the two remaining resolutions and the bill recommended by the majority to the House. And particularly does he dissent from the third and last resolution in the report of the majority; regarding it as asserting a principle which, if carried out in practice, would virtually vest the entire power of appointment to and removal from office in the Senate, and in fact the whole executive power of the Government; a result which, in his belief, the framers of the Constitution never contemplated, which is against the contemporaneous exposition given to that instrument, and which would, in effect, constitute the Senate the supervisor and dictator of the Executive, and end in that concentration of power in one branch of the Government which the faithful and vigilant patriot has ever feared and sought to avoid. The undersigned might go into an elaborate argument to sustain his views in relation to the subjects submitted by the majority, but he at present contents himself with the simple expression of his opinion, and his dissent from that part of the report, and the resolutions and bill, of the majority, to which he has above referred.

EDMUND BURKE.

IN THE SENATE OF THE UNITED STATES.

MARCH 1, 1886.—Ordered to be printed.

Mr. PUGH, from the Committee on the Judiciary, submitted the following

VIEWS OF THE MINORITY

ON THE

LETTER OF THE ATTORNEY-GENERAL OF THE UNITED STATES DECLINING TO TRANSMIT TO THE SENATE COPIES OF OFFICIAL RECORDS AND PAPERS CONCERNING THE ADMINISTRATION OF THE OFFICE OF THE DISTRICT ATTORNEY OF THE SOUTHERN DISTRICT OF ALABAMA.

The minority of the Committee on the Judiciary, to whom was referred a letter from the Attorney-General of the United States declining to transmit to the Senate copies of official records and papers concerning the administration of the office of the district attorney of the southern district of Alabama from January 1, 1885, to January 25, 1886, respectfully submit the following report:

When President Cleveland came into office he found at least 95 per cent. of the civil offices of the United States filled by Republicans, who had enjoyed their honors and emoluments through a period of twenty years, and as a rule these public positions had been distributed as rewards for partisan service, which the recipients continued to render after their appointment.

The President was elected on the declaration that civil office was a public trust, to be so treated by incumbents in practice, as well as in theory, and also upon the conviction of a majority of the people that it was a standing menace to the honesty, purity, and safety of the Government to perpetuate in these offices partisan officials who had procured their positions by partisan service, and employed their emoluments, power, and influence for personal gain, and as aids in securing party supremacy.

The party to whom the President owes his nomination and election had been exiled from all participation in the civil administration of the Government for nearly a quarter of a century, and it seemed reasonable and just that the five millions of voters who had been thus politically ostracized should be allowed at least a fair share of the offices which had been created for the benefit of the whole people, without regard to party divisions. The friends and supporters of the President made application to him for a redistribution of the public trusts under the Government, so that they might receive, not as the spoils of victory, but as public honors and emoluments, at least a fair share of what was then monopolized by his political opponents, who were and had been unfriendly to Democratic principles and could not be trusted as agents to promote the usefulness and success of Democratic administration.

No other President has ever been subjected to such severe trial or had to meet so many grave difficulties since he entered upon the discharge of the duties of his high office. No other President has ever had, in quantity or quality, such an abundant supply of valid reasons and causes urging him to a free exercise of his power of removal from Federal office; and no other President ever resisted with more firmness the just claims of his supporters, or used his power of removal more conscientiously, cautiously, and sparingly. Nearly twelve months have elapsed since the President's inauguration, and six hundred and fifty will more than cover the whole number of removals or suspensions. Had the number reached as many thousands as hundreds he would not by this time have made an equal division between the two national parties of the offices not embraced in the civil-service law.

Notwithstanding these undeniable facts and circumstances, the six hundred and fifty nominations sent to the Senate in the suspension cases made during the recess of the Senate have been allowed to remain before the committees without consideration and final disposition. In the able and ingenious report of the majority of the committee the Senate and the country are informed for the first time of the grounds and reasons for such long delay and non-action. The basis and justification for this remarkable procedure by which suspension cases are to be postponed an indefinite period, and important legislative business interrupted, and no purpose served but to agitate and distract the public mind, is the suspension of Duskin from the powers and duties of the office of district attorney of the southern district of Alabama, whose term of office has long since expired, and the nomination of Burnett to take the place. Duskin has made no complaint to the Judiciary Committee, the Senate, the President, or the Attorney-General that he was wronged by the suspension. The Judiciary Committee is in possession of full information showing that Burnett was recommended to the President by all the members of Congress from Alabama, on personal knowledge of his high character and qualifications for the office, and that since he has been in the discharge of its duties he has the unqualified indorsement of the judge and clerk of the district court of the United States, both Republicans.

The resolution of the Senate directs the Attorney-General " to transmit to the Senate copies of all documents and papers that have been filed in the Department of Justice since the 1st day of January, 1885, in relation to the management and conduct of the office of the district attorney of the United States for the southern district of Alabama." The answer of the Attorney-General is :

"That the papers and documents which are mentioned in said resolution and still remaining in the custody of the Department have exclusive reference to the suspension by the President of George M. Duskin, the late incumbent of the office of district attorney for the southern district of Alabama, and it is not considered that the public interest will be promoted by a compliance with said resolution and the transmission of the papers and documents therein mentioned to the Senate in executive session."

Stript to the naked truth, without any special pleading, the case made for the decision of the Senate on their resolution, and the answer of the Attorney-General is, whether the Senate has the right to demand of the Attorney-General the transmission, against the order of the President, of the only paper or document of the description mentioned in the resolution, when that paper or document is stated in the refusal to relate exclusively to the removal of Duskin by the President, and for that reason alone not transmitted. The paper shows on its face to what it relates, and it requires the exercise of no judgment to determine its character. The President holds that it is not a public document, and there can be no doubt about the correctness of his decision, which must be accepted as conclusive.

It is an undeniable truth, without qualification or exception in any case, that every right, power, privilege, or prerogative created by any law, or granted in the Constitution to Congress, or any Department or officer of the Government, has some just reason, use, necessity, or foundation for its existence and support. The majority of the Judiciary Committee in their report affirm the right of the Senate in executive session, or in open session, to direct the Attorney-General or any head of a Department, or to request the President to transmit to the Senate, in open or executive session, *any paper* on the files of the Department or in the possession of the President, *if such paper relates to an "official act" of the President or the head of any Department,* although such "official act" is the removal or suspension by the President of a civil officer of the United States.

The minority deny that the claim of the majority of the committee in the case now before the Senate, or in any case where the paper or document relates exclusively or materially to removals or suspensions by the President, has any foundation or recognition to support it in the Constitution, or any valid law, custom, or precedent. The burden rests upon the majority of the committee of showing that the right or power exists in the Senate, under the Constitution, or some law, custom, or precedent, and the reason, use, or necessity for it, to direct the head of any Department, or to request the President to send to the Senate, in open or executive session, any paper, or document, in the President's possession, or on the files of any of the Departments, not public, but relating exclusively, or materially, to his official act of removal or suspension of a civil officer of the United States.

It is difficult for the minority to decide what unmistakable rights powers, or prerogatives are claimed for the Senate in the report of the majority that are controverted in this proceeding, or that have any bearing, application, or significance whatsoever to the real issue joined between the Senate and the President. The committee seems to think that it strengthens their claim to the papers and documents in question that the order to transmit them is made by the Senate upon the head of a department. It is broadly asserted in the majority report that "it is within the constitutional competency of either House of Congress to have access to the *official papers* and *documents* in the various public offices." If it is not intended by the majority that this "constitutional competency of either House of Congress to have access to official papers and documents in the various public offices" should embrace papers and documents relating exclusively to removals and suspensions by the President, why make the claim of right in the two Houses so sweeping and comprehensive?

It is admitted in the majority report that no statute confers the right on either House to direct the Attorney-General to send to either House any official papers and documents, but the committee claims that the right exists "as a necessary incident from the very nature of the powers intrusted by the Constitution to the two Houses of Congress"; "that either House must have at all times the right to know all that officially exists or takes place in any of the Departments of the Government." Can any grant of power in the Constitution to either House of Congress be found "that in its very nature requires that either House should have at all times the right to know anything, wherever or in whatever form it may exist, about removals or suspensions of Federal officers by the President ?"

The minority admit, once for all, that any and every public document, paper, or record on the files of any Department, or in the possession of the President, relating to any subject whatever, over which either house of Congress has any grant of power, jurisdiction, or control under the Constitution, is subject to the call or inspection of either house for use in the exercise of its constitutional powers and jurisdiction.   It is on this clearly-defined and well-founded constitutional principle that, wherever any power is lodged by the Constitution, all incidents follow such power that are necessary and proper to enable the custodian of it to carry it into execution.   Whether the power is granted to Congress, or either house, or to the President, or any Department or officer of the Government, or to the President by and with the advice and consent of the Senate, the principle is as fundamental as the Constitution itself that all the necessary incidents of such grants accompany the grants and belong to and can be exercised by the custodians of such powers, jointly or severally, as they may be vested by the Constitution.

It is on the application and enforcement of this unquestioned rule of construction that either house of Congress has the right inherent in the power itself to direct the head of any Department, or request the President to transmit any information in the knowledge of either, or any public or official papers or documents, or their contents, on the files or in the keeping of either, *provided* such papers or documents relate to subjects, matters, or things in the consideration of which the house making the call can use such information, papers, or documents in the exercise of any right, power, jurisdiction, or privilege granted to Congress, or either house, or to the President by and with the advice and consent of the Senate.

But if all the power granted in the Constitution over the subject-matter or thing to which papers or documents relate, wherever they may be found, is vested by the Constitution in the President exclusively, the only rightful custodian of all such papers or documents, or the information they contain, is the chief executive officer, to whom the Constitution has intrusted all the power its framers were willing to grant over that subject.   It would be a reflection upon the common sense of the framers of the Constitution to decide that they had vested in the President and the Senate all the power to make and ratify treaties, and while withholding from the House of Representatives all such power, they had granted, by implication, to the House of Representatives the right to have access to all the papers and documents upon which the President and Senate had acted in making and ratifying treaties.

Why was the possession or inspection of such papers and documents by the House of Representatives refused by President Washington ? For the plain reason that the House of Representatives had no power over treaty-making.   It would be equally unreasonable to conclude that the framers of the Constitution had declined to divide the power of removing Federal officers between the President and Senate, and after vesting all such greater power of removal (if it has been done) in the President alone, they should at the same time give to the Senate, by implication, or as a necessary incident of another power, the less right of advising and consenting to removals.   That would amount to vesting the principal power of removal in the President, and imposing a limitation upon it, to be found as a mere incident of another and different power of advising and consenting to appointments.

The view enforced by the minority in this report of the vital and paramount question presented from the committee to the Senate, makes it unnecessary to notice the attempt of the majority to make something out of the fact that the resolution of the Senate is directed to the Attorney-General, and that as he is an officer created by a law of Congress either house has just as much power over him as the President, except to say that if such reasoning is sound it would compel the Secretary of State to transmit to the House of Representatives on its order all papers and documents relating to the making and ratifying of treaties on file in the State Department, which is also the creation of a law of Congress. Besides, the effort to place the duty of transmitting the papers called for to the Senate upon the head of a Department, as separate and distinct from the President, or to say this is not the act of the President, is not permissible.

The President speaks or acts through the heads of the several Departments in relation to subjects which appertain to their respective duties. This principle is recognized by the Supreme Court in Wilcox v. Jackson, 13 Peters, 513, and many subsequent decisions.

Without circumlocution, or evasion, or generalizing, or dealing in subtilities, or refining on irrelevant and misleading cases cited in the majority report, the minority of your committee, after making as diligent a search as time and opportunity allowed, feel satisfied that from 1789 to 1867, a period of seventy-eight years, not a single case can be found, and not a single case occurred in which the Senate in executive session, by resolution or otherwise, directed the head of any Department, or requested the President to transmit to the Senate in executive session papers or documents on file, or in the custody of the head of the Department, or the President, relating exclusively or materially to removals of Federal officers by the President during the recess or the sessions of the Senate, and such resolution was obeyed by any head of a Department or the President.

To meet the case squarely, the minority feel the utmost confidence in stating that, during a period of seventy-eight years, from 1789 to 1867, no such resolution as that now before the Senate was ever obeyed by the President or any head of a Department. The majority of the committee says:

The instances of requests to the President and commands to the heads of Departments by each house of Congress from those days until now for papers and information on every conceivable subject of public affairs are almost innumerable; for it appears to have been thought by all the Presidents who have carried on the Government now for almost a century, that even in respect of requests to them, an independent co-ordinate branch of the Government, they were under a constitutional duty and obligation to furnish to either house the papers called for, unless, as has happened in very rare instances, when the request was coupled with an appeal to the discretion of the President in respect to the danger of publicity to send the papers, if, in his judgment, it should not be incompatible with the public welfare.

Is this broad statement made as an authority for the call on the Attorney-General to send to the Senate in executive session the papers in his Department relating exclusively to the suspension of Duskin by the President? If not, what purpose is intended to be served by the statement? If intended to sustain the present call on the Attorney-General, would it not be a remarkable coincidence that Washington, who signed the act of Congress declaratory of the exclusive right of the President to make removals, and Madison, whose matchless powers were devoted to the passage of that act, intended as he declared in the debate as a "permanent settlement of the constitutional power of the President to make removals within his discretion without accountability to the Senate," to obey requests, or for his cabinet officers to obey demands for the transmission of papers to the Senate in Executive session, or to either house in open session, relating exclusively to an "official act" of removal, over which he believed he had been instrusted with the sole power by the Constitution? And would it not be equally inexplicable that such a request or demand would have been obeyed by John Quincy Adams, or by Andrew Jackson, "in times of the highest party excitement and stress," in 1826 and 1835? If Adams and Jackson were willing to obey such requests and demands or ever did so, why did Mr. Benton in 1826 and Mr. Calhoun in 1835 report bills to the Senate requiring the President to transmit to the Senate the cause of removals and the papers relating thereto, which bills fell still-born, on the table of the Senate.

It is not true that a single precedent can be found for a continuous period of seventy eight years that gives any support whatever to the present demand of the Senate upon the Attorney-General to transmit papers relating exclusively to the removal of Duskin. Every precedent cited in the report of the majority has for its foundation the constitutional power of the Senate to participate with the President in the official act to which the papers called for related. The Senate shares with the President the treaty-making power, and he can make no appointment to office without the advice and consent of the Senate. Upon the subjects of treaty-making and appointments, papers relating thereto, when requested or demanded, have been sent to the Senate, for the plain reason that the President and Senate are jointly intrusted with powers in relation to treaties and appointments which the Senate cannot safely and wisely exercise without the inspection of papers and documents relating thereto in the Departments or in the keeping of the President. No such foundation, reason, or necessity exists in the matter of removals from office.

The demand in the present case upon the Attorney-General, and its persistent pressure by the majority of the committee, after he has declined, on the order of the President, to obey it, for the sole reason that the only papers in his Department, filed there since January 1, 1885, relate *exclusively* to the removal of Duskin by the President, *necessarily implies* that in the judgment of a majority of the committee the Senate has the same constitutional power over removals that it has over appointments—that is, the power of advising and consenting thereto. There is no escape from this crucial test of who is in the right in this controversy, the Senate or the President.

The question is the same as that presented in the First Congress in 1789; revived in the Senate in 1826; pressed again in the Senate in 1835; revived again in 1867, when the President was hampered by unconstitutional legislation forced through Congress by a revolutionary majority under the pressure of overruling party necessity; soon revived again by President Grant in 1869, and ending in reactionary legislation, restoring the power and calling it "suspension" from office, to the "*discretion*" of the President, and thereby conferring upon him the power, if he wills to exercise it, of expelling permanently from office any incumbent, with or without cause, and in defiance of any power in the Senate to prevent the President from making the suspension perpetual. The same old struggle again comes up in this Senate without provocation, or any meritorious excuse or justification. In self-defense the President and the friends of his constitutional prerogative in the Senate are again forced to meet and answer the question,

Where does the power of making removals from Federal office reside? Does the Constitution answer this question? All it says is:

(1) The executive power shall be vested in a President of the United States of America.

(2) He shall have power, by and with the advice and consent of the Senate, to make treaties, provided two-thirds of the Senators present concur; and he shall nominate and, by and with the advice and consent of the Senate, shall appoint ambassadors, other public ministers and consuls, judges of the Supreme Court, and all other officers of the United States whose appointments are not herein otherwise provided for, and which shall be established by law; but the Congress may by law vest the appointment of such inferior officers as they think proper in the President alone, in the courts of law, or in the heads of Departments.

(3) The President shall have power to fill up all vacancies that may happen during the recess of the Senate by granting commissions which shall expire at the end of their next session.

(4) He shall take care that the laws be faithfully executed, and shall commission all the officers of the United States.

The question of the meaning of the above quotations from the Constitution, and what disposition, if any, they make of the power of removing officers of the United States, came up for consideration and settlement by the First Congress in May, 1789. There were many framers of the Constitution in that Congress, and none of them had more to do in that great work or were more familiar with its meaning than Mr. Madison. This debate, considered the most remarkable in the history of Congress, is published in "Annals of Congress," 1789, vol. 1, from pages 372 to 585.

The minority of your committee is satisfied that they are unable to produce anything themselves, or from others, that can add to what was said in that famous debate on the question reported to the Senate. The decision was made by statesmen fresh from the work of framing the Constitution, and at a time when no political parties had been organized to influence judgment and control opinion. No settlement of any controverted question ever had higher sanctions or more to commend it to unquestioned acquiescence.

Said Mr. Madison:

However various the opinions which exist upon the point now before us, it seems agreed on all sides that it demands a careful investigation and full discussion. I feel the importance of the question, and know that our decision will involve the decision of all similar cases. The decision that is at this time made will become the permanent exposition of the Constitution; and on a permanent exposition of the Constitution will depend the genius and character of the whole Government.

The following are extracts from some of the speeches made on that memorable occasion:

Mr. Madison said:

I think it absolutely necessary that the President should have the power of removing from office; it will make him, in a peculiar manner, responsible for their conduct and subject him to impeachment himself, if he suffers them to perpetrate with impunity high crimes or misdemeanors against the United States or neglects to superintend their conduct so as to check their excesses. On the constitutionality of the declaration I have no manner of doubt.

It is said that it comports with the nature of things that those who appoint should have the power of removal; but I cannot conceive that this sentiment is warranted by the Constitution. I believe it would be found very inconvenient in practice. It is one of the most prominent features of the Constitution—a principle that pervades the whole system—that there should be the highest possible degree of responsibility in all the executive officers thereof. Anything, therefore, which tends to lessen this responsibility is contrary to its spirit and intention, and, unless it is saddled upon us expressly by the letter of that work, I shall oppose the admission of it into any act of the legislature.

Now, if the heads of the Executive Departments are subjected to removal by the President, we have in him security for the good behavior of the officer. If he does not conform to the judgment of the President in doing the executive duties of his office, he can be displaced. This makes him responsible to the great Executive power, and makes the President responsible to the public for the conduct of the person he has nominated and appointed to aid him in the administration of his Department. But if the President shall join in a collusion with this officer, and continue a bad man in office, the case of impeachment will reach the culprit and drag him forth to punishment.

But if you take the other construction, and say he shall not be displaced but by and with the advice and consent of the Senate, the President is no longer answerable for the conduct of the officer; all will depend upon the Senate. You here destroy a real responsibility without obtaining even the shadow; for no gentleman will pretend to say the responsibility of the Senate can be of such a nature as to afford substantial security. But why, it may be asked, was the Senate joined with the President in appointing to office, if they have no responsibility? I answer, merely for the sake of advising, being supposed, from their nature, better acquainted with the character of the candidates than an individual; yet even here the President is held to the responsibility—he nominates, and, with their consent, appoints. No person can be forced upon him as an assistant by any other branch of the Government.

There is another objection to this construction, which I consider of some weight, and shall therefore mention to the committee. Perhaps there was no argument urged with more success, or more plausibly grounded against the Constitution, under which we are now deliberating. than than that founded on the mingling of the executive and legislative branches of the Government in one body. It has been objected that the Senate have too much of the executive power even by having a control over the President in the appointment to office.

Now, shall we extend this connection between the legislative and executive Departments, which will strengthen the objection, and diminish the responsibility we have in the head of the Executive?

Mr. Sedgwick (vol. 1, First Congress, p. 460):

But they say the Senate is to be united with the President in the exercise of this power. I hope, sir, this is not the case, because it would involve us in the most serious difficulty. Suppose a discovery of any of those events which I have just enumerated were to take place when the Senate is not in session, how is the remedy to be applied? This is a serious consideration, and the evil could be avoided no other way than by the Senate's sitting always. Surely no gentleman of this House contemplates the necessity of incurring such an expense. I am sure it will be very objectionable to our constituents; and yet this must be done, or the public interest be endangered by keeping an unworthy officer in place until that body shall be assembled from the extremes of the Union.

It has been said that there is danger of this power being abused, if exercised by one man. Certainly the danger is as great with respect to the Senate, who are assembled from various parts of the continent, with different impressions and opinions. It appears to me that such a body is more likely to misuse this power than the man whom the united voice of America calls to the Presidential chair. As the nature of the Government requires the power of removal, I think it is to be exercised in this way by a hand capable of exerting itself with effect, and the power must be conferred upon the President by the Constitution, as the executive officer of the Government.

Mr. Madison said (page 463):

The Constitution affirms that the executive power shall be vested in the President. Are there exceptions to this proposition? Yes; there are. The Constitution says that in appointing to office the Senate shall be associated with the President, unless in the case of inferior officers, when the law shall otherwise direct. Have we a right to extend this exception? I believe not. If the Constitution has invested all executive power in the President, I venture to assert that the legislature has no right to diminish or modify his executive authority. The question now resolves itself into this: Is the power of displacing an executive power? I conceive that if any power whatsoever is in its nature executive, it is the power of appointing, overseeing, and controlling those who execute the laws.

If the Constitution had not qualified the power of the President in appointing to office, by associating the Senate with him in that business, would it not be clear that he would have the right, by virtue of his executive power, to make such appointment? Should we be authorized, in defiance of that clause in the Constitution, "The executive power shall be vested in a President," to unite the Senate with the President in the appointment to office? I conceive not. If it is admitted that we should not be authorized to do this, I think it may be disputed whether we have a right to associate them in removing persons from office, the one power being as much of an executive nature as the other; and the first only is authorized by being excepted out of the general rule established by the Constitution in these words, "The executive power shall be vested in the President."

The judicial power is vested in a Supreme Court; but will gentlemen say the judicial power can be placed elsewhere unless the Constitution has made an exception? The Constitution justifies the Senate in exercising a judiciary power in determining on impeachments; but can the judicial power be further blended with the powers of that body? They cannot. I therefore say it is incontrovertible, if neither the legislative nor judicial powers are subjected to qualifications other than those demanded in the Constitution, that the executive powers are equally unabatable as either of the others; and inasmuch as the power of removal is of an executive nature, and not affected by any Constitutional exception, it is beyond the reach of the legislative body.

Mr. Clymer said (p. 489):

If I were to give my vote merely on constitutional ground, I should be totally indifferent whether the words were struck out or not; because I am clear that the Executive has the power of removal as incident to his department; and, if the Constitution had been silent with respect to the appointment, he would have had that power also. The reason, perhaps, why it was mentioned in the Constitution, was to give some further security against the introduction of improper men into office. But in cases of removal there is not such necessity for this check. What great danger would arise from the removal of a worthy man, when the Senate must be consulted in the appointment of his successor? Is it likely they will consent to advance an improper character? The presumption therefore is, that he would not abuse this power; or, if he did, only one good man would be changed for another.

If the President is divested of his power, his responsibility is destroyed; you prevent his efficiency, and disable him from affording security to the people which the Constitution contemplates. What use will it be of to call the citizens of the Union together every four years to obtain a purified choice of a representative, if he is to be a mere cipher in the Government? The Executive must act by others; but you reduce him to a mere shadow, when you control both the power of appointment and removal; if you take away the latter power, he ought to resign the power of superintending and directing the executive parts of Government into the hands of the Senate at once, and then we become a dangerous aristocracy, or shall be more destitute of energy than any Government on earth. These being my sentiments, I wish the clause to stand as a legislative declaration, that the power of removal is constitutionally vested in the President.

Mr. Madison said (p. 495):

However various the opinions which exist upon the point now before us, it seems agreed on all sides that it demands a careful investigation and full discussion. I feel the importance of the question, and know that our decision will involve the decision of all similar cases. The decision that is at this time made will become the permanent exposition of the Constitution, and on a permanent exposition of the Constitution will depend the genius and character of the whole Government. It will depend, perhaps, on this decision whether the Government shall retain that equilibrium which the Constitution intended, or take a direction towards aristocracy or anarchy among the members of the Government. Hence, how careful ought we be to give a true direction to a power so critically circumstanced.

It is incumbent on us to weigh with particular attention the arguments which have been advanced in support of the various opinions with cautious deliberation. I own to you, Mr. Chairman, that I feel great anxiety upon this question. I feel an anxiety because I am called upon to give a decision in a case that may affect the fundamental principles of the Government under which we act, and liberty itself. But all that I can do on such an occasion is to weigh well everything advanced on both sides with the purest desire to find out the true meaning of the Constitution, and to be guided by that and an attachment to the true spirit of liberty, whose influence I believe strongly predominates here.

Several constructions have been put upon the Constitution relative to the point in question. The gentleman from Connecticut (Mr. Sherman) has advanced a doctrine which was not touched upon before. He seems to think (if I understood him rightly) that the power of displacing from office is subject to legislative discretion; because it, having a right to create, it may limit or modify as it thinks proper. I shall not say but at first view this doctrine may seem to have some plausibility; but when I consider that the Constitution clearly intended to maintain a marked distinction between the legislative, executive, and judicial powers of Government; and when I consider that if the legislature has a power such as is contended for, they may subject and transfer at discretion powers from one Department of our Government to another, they may, on that principle, exclude the President altogether from exercising any authority in the removal of officers; they may give it to the Senate alone, or the President and Senate combined; they may vest it in the whole Congress, or they may reserve it to be exercised by this House. When I consider the consequences of this doctrine, and compare them with the true principles of the Constitution, I own that I cannot subscribe to it.

The doctrine, however, which seems to stand most in opposition to the principles I contend for, is, that the power to name an appointment is, in the nature of things, incidental to the power which makes the appointment. I agree that if nothing more was said in the Constitution than that the President, by and with the advice and consent of the Senate, should appoint to office, there would be a great force in saying that the power of removal resulted by a natural implication from the power of appointing. But there is another part of the Constitution no less explicit than the one on which the gentleman's doctrine is founded. It is that part which declares that the executive power shall be vested in a President of the United States. The association of the Senate with the President in exercising that particular function is an exception to this general rule; and exceptions to general rules, I conceive, are ever to be taken strictly.

But there is another part of the Constitution which inclines, in my judgment, to favor the construction I put upon it; the President is required to take care that the laws be faithfully executed. If the duty to see the laws faithfully executed be required at the hands of the Executive Magistrate, it would seem that it was generally intended he should have that species of power which is necessary to accomplish that end. Now, if the officer when once appointed is not to depend upon the President for his official existence, but upon a distinct body (for where there are two negatives required, either can prevent the removal), I confess I do not see how the President can take care that the laws be faithfully executed. It is true, by a circuitous operation he may obtain in impeachment, and even without this it is possible he may obtain the concurrence of the Senate for the purpose of displacing an officer; but would this give that species of control to the Executive Magistrate which seems to be required by the Constitution?

I own, if my opinion was not contrary to that entertained by what I suppose to be the minority on this question, I should be doubtful of being mistaken when I discovered how inconsistent that construction would make the Constitution with itself. I can hardly bring myself to imagine the wisdom of the convention who framed the Constitution contemplated such incongruity.

There is another maxim which ought to direct us in expounding the Constitution, and is of great importance. It is laid down in most of the constitutions or bills of rights in the republics of America; it is to be found in the political writings of the most celebrated civilians, and is every where held as essential to the preservation of liberty, that the three great departments of Government be kept separate and distinct; and if in any case they are blended, it is in order to admit a partial qualification, in order more effectually to guard against an entire consolidation.

I think, therefore, when we review the several parts of this Constitution where it says that the legislative powers shall be vested in a Congress of the United States, under certain exceptions, and the executive powers vested in the President with certain exceptions, we must suppose they were intended to be kept separate in all cases in which they are not blended, and ought, consequently, to expound the Constitution so as to blend them as little as possible. Everything relative to the merits of the question, as distinguished from a constitutional question, seems to turn on the danger of such a power vested in the President alone; but when I consider the checks under which he lies in the exercise of this power, I own to you I feel no apprehension but what arise from the dangers incidental to the power itself, for dangers will be incidental to it vest it where you please.

I will not reiterate what was said before with respect to the mode of election, and the extreme improbability that any citizen will be selected from the mass of citizens who is not highly distinguished by his abilities and worth; in this alone we have no small security for the faithful exercise of this power. But, throwing that out of the question, let us consider the restraints he will feel after he is placed in that elevated station. It is to be remarked that the power in this case will not consist so much in continuing a bad man in office as in the danger of displacing a good one. Perhaps the great danger, as has been observed, of abuse in the executive power lies in the improper continuance of bad men in office. But the power we contend for will not enable him to do this; for if an unworthy man be continued in office by an unworthy President, the House of Representatives can at any time impeach him, and the Senate can remove him, whether the President chooses or not.

The danger then consists merely in this: The President can displace from office a man whose merits require that he should be continued in it. What will be the motives which the President can feel for such abuse of his power, and the restraints that operate to prevent it? In the first place, he will be impeachable by this House before the Senate for such an act of maladministration; for I contend that the wanton removal of meritorious officers would subject him to impeachment and removal from his own high trust. But what can be his motives for displacing a worthy man? It must be that he may fill the place with an unworthy creature of his own. Can he accomplish this end? No; he can place no man in the vacancy whom the Senate shall not approve; and, if he could fill the vacancy with the man he might choose, I am sure he would have little inducement to make an improper removal. Let us consider the consequences. The injured man will be supported by the popular opinion: the community will take sides with him against the President: it will facilitate those combinations and give success to those exertions which will be pursued to prevent his re-election.

To displace a man of high merit, and who from his station may be supposed a man of extensive influence, are considerations in the mind of any man who may fill the Presidential chair. The friends of those individuals and the public sympathy will be against him. If this should not produce his impeachment before the Senate, it will amount to an impeachment before the community, who will have the power of punishment, by refusing to re-elect him. But suppose this persecuted individual cannot obtain revenge in this mode, there are other modes in which he could make the situation of the President very inconvenient, if you suppose him resolutely bent on executing the dictates of resentment. If he had not influence enough to direct the vengeance of the whole community, he may probably be able to obtain an appointment in one or the other branch of the legislature, and, being a man of weight, talents, and influence, in either case he may prove to the President troublesome indeed.

We have seen examples in the history of other nations which justifies the remark I now have made. Though the prerogatives of the British King are great as his rank, and it is unquestionably known that he has a positive influence over both branches of the legislative body, yet there have been examples in which the appointment and removal of ministers have been found to be dictated by one or other of those branches. Now, if this be the case with an hereditary monarch possessed of those high prerogatives and furnished with so many means of influence, can we suppose a President, elected for four years only, dependent upon the popular voice, impeachable by the legislature, little, if at all, distinguished for wealth, personal talents, or influence from the head of the Department himself, I say will he bid defiance to all these considerations, and wantonly dismiss a meritorious and virtuous officer? Such abuse of power exceeds my conception. If anything takes place in the ordinary course of business of this kind, my imagination cannot extend to it on any rational principle.

But let us not consider the question on one side only; there are dangers to be contemplated on the other. Vest this power in the Senate jointly with the President, and you abolish at once that great principle of unity and responsibility in the executive department which was intended for the security of liberty and the public good. If the President should possess alone the power of removal from office, those who are employed in the execution of the law will be in their proper situation, and the claim of dependence be preserved; the lowest officers, the middle grade, and the highest will depend, as they ought, on the President, and the President on the community. The chain of dependence, therefore, terminates in the supreme body, namely, in the people, who will possess, besides, in aid of their original power, the decisive engine of impeachment.

Take the other supposition, that the power should be vested in the Senate, on the principle that the power to displace is necessarily connected with the power to appoint. It is declared by the Constitution that we may by law vest the appointment of inferior officers in the heads of Departments; the power of removal being incidental, as stated by some gentlemen. Where does this terminate? If you begin with the subordinate officers, they are dependents, on their superior, he on the next superior, and he on—whom? On the Senate, a permanent body; a body by its particular mode of election in reality existing forever; a body possessing that proportion of aristocratic power which the Constitution no doubt thought wise to be established in the system, but which some have strongly excepted against.

And let me ask, gentlemen, is there equal security in this case as in the other? Shall we trust the Senate, responsible to individual legislatures, rather than the person who is responsible to the whole community? It is true, the Senate do not hold their offices for life, like aristocracies recorded in the historic page; yet the fact is, they will not possess that responsibility for the exercise of executive powers which would render it safe for us to vest such powers in them. But what an aspect will this give to the Executive? Instead of keeping the departments of the Government distinct, you make an Executive out of one branch of the legislature; you make the Executive a two-headed monster, to use the expression of the gentleman from New Hampshire (Mr. Livermore); you destroy the great principle of responsibility, and perhaps have the creature divided in its will, defeating the very purposes for which a unity in the Executive was instituted.

These objections do not lie against such an arrangement as the bill establishes. I conceive that the President is sufficiently accountable to the community, and if this power is vested in him it will be vested where its nature requires it should be vested; if anything in its nature is executive, it must be that power which is employed in superintending and seeing that the laws are faithfully executed. The laws cannot be executed but by officers appointed for that purpose; therefore, those who are over such officers naturally possess the executive power. If any other doctrine be admitted, what is the consequence? You may set the Senate at the head of the executive department, or you may require that the officers hold their places during the pleasure of this branch of the legislature, if you cannot go so far as to say we shall appoint them, and by this means you link together two branches of the Government which the preservation of liberty requires to be constantly separated.

The following are the judicial recognitions and sanctions of the validity and binding character of the settlement made of this great question in 1789. Chancellor Kent, in his Commentaries, vol. 1, 10th ed., p. 346, uses the following language:

This [meaning the settlement in 1789] amounted to a legislative construction of the Constitution, and it has ever since been acquiesced in and acted upon, as of decisive authority in the case. It applies equally to every other officer of Government appointed by the President and Senate whose term of duration is not specially declared. It is supported by the weighty reason that the subordinate officers in the executive department ought to hold at the pleasure of the head of that department, because he is invested generally with the executive authority, and every participation in that authority by the Senate was an exception to a general principle and ought to be taken strictly. The President is the great responsible officer for the faithful execution of the law, and the power of removal was incidental to that duty and might often be requisite to fulfill it. It may now be considered as firmly and definitely settled, and there is good sense and practical utility in the construction.

The Supreme Court of the United States, in Ex parte Hennen (13 Peters, p. 259), says:

It was very early adopted as the practical construction of the Constitution that the power of removal was vested in the President alone, and such would appear to have been the legislative construction of the Constitution. For in the organization of the three great Departments of State, War, and Treasury, in the year 1789, provision is made for the appointment of a subordinate officer by the head of the Department, who should have the charge and custody of the records, books, and papers appertaining to the office, when the head of the Department should be removed from the office of the President of the United States. (1 Story, 5, 31, 47.)

When the Navy Department was established, in the year 1798 (1 Story, 498), provision is made for the charge and custody of the books, records, and documents of the Department, in case of vacancy in the office of Secretary by removal or otherwise. It is not here said, by removal by the President, as is done with respect to the heads of the other Departments; and yet there can be no doubt that he holds his office by the same tenure as the other Secretaries, and is removable by the President. The change of phraseology arose probably from its having become the settled and well-understood construction of the Constitution that the power of removal was vested in the President alone in such cases, although the appointment of the officer was by the President and Senate.

Again, the Supreme Court of the United States, in Blake's case (U. S. Reports, Vol. 103, p. 232), quoted approvingly its antecedent decision, in the following language:

But it was very early adopted as the practical construction of the Constitution that this power was vested in the President alone. And such would appear to have been the legislative construction of the Constitution.

In Kilbourn v. Thompson (103 U. S. Rep.) the identical principles involved in the present conflict between the Senate and President are elaborately considered and decided.

Justice Miller, delivering the opinion of the court, said:

It is believed to be one of the chief merits of the American system of written Constitutional law, that all the powers intrusted to government, whether state or national, are divided into the three grand departments—the executive, the legislative, and the judicial.

That the functions appropriate to each of these branches of government shall be vested in a separate body of public servants, and that the perfection of the system requires that the lines which separate and divide these departments shall be broadly and clearly defined. It is also essential to the successful working of this system that the persons intrusted with power in any one of these branches shall not be permitted to encroach upon the powers confided to the others, but that each shall by the law of its creation be limited to the exercise of the powers appropriate to its own department and no other.

To these general propositions there are in the Constitution of the United States some important exceptions. One of these is, that the President is so far made a part of the legislative power that his assent is required to the enactment of all statutes and resolutions of Congress. This, however, is so only to a limited extent, for a bill may become a law notwithstanding the refusal of the President to approve it, by a vote of two-thirds of each house of Congress. So, also, the Senate is made a partaker in the functions of appointing officers and making treaties, which are supposed to be properly executive, by requiring its consent to the appointment of such officers and the ratification of treaties. The Senate also exercises the judicial power of trying impeachment, and the House of preferring articles of impeachment.

In the main, however, that instrument, the model on which are constructed the fundamental laws of the States, has blocked out with singular precision, and in bold lines, in its three primary articles, the allotment of power to the executive, the legislative, and the judicial departments of the Government. It also remains true, as a general rule, that the powers confided by the Constitution to one of these departments *cannot* be exercised by another. It may be said that these are truisms which need no repetition here to give them force. But while the experience of almost a century has in general shown a wise and commendable forbearance in each of these branches from encroachments upon the others, it is not to be denied that such attempts have been made, and it is believed not always without success.

The increase in the number of States, in their population and wealth, and in the amount of power, if not in its nature, to be exercised by the Federal Government, presents powerful and growing temptation to those to whom that exercise is intrusted to overstep the just boundaries of their own department and enter upon the domain of one of the others, or to assume powers not intrusted to either of them.

The House of Representatives, having the exclusive right to originate all bills for raising revenue, whether by taxation or otherwise; having, with the Senate, the right to declare war, and fix the compensation of all officers and servants of the Government, and vote the supplies which must pay that compensation; and being also the most numerous body of all those engaged in the exercise of the primary powers of the Government, is for these reasons least of all liable to encroachment upon its appropriate domain. By reason, also, of its popular origin, and the frequency with which the short term of office of its members requires the renewal of their authority at the hands of the people—the great source of all power in this country—encroachments by that body on the domain of co-ordinate branches of the Government would be received with less distrust than a similar exercise of unwarranted power by any other department of the Government. It is all the more necessary, therefore, that the exercise of power by this body, when acting separately from and independently of all other depositories of power, should be watched with vigilance, and when called in question before any other tribunal having the right to pass upon it, that it should receive the most careful scrutiny.

In looking to the preamble and resolution under which the committee acted, before which Kilbourn refused to testify, we are of opinion that [the House of Representatives not only exceeded the limits of its own authority, but assumed a power which could only be properly exercised by another branch of the Government, because it was in its nature clearly judicial.

The Constitution declares that the judicial power of the United States shall be vested in one Supreme Court, and in such inferior courts as the Congress may from time to time ordain and establish. If what we have said of the division of the powers of the Government among the three departments be sound, this is equivalent to a declaration that no judicial power is vested in the Congress or either branch of it, save in the cases specifically enumerated, to which we have referred. If the investigation which the committee was directed to make was judicial in its character, and could only be properly and successfully made by a court of justice, and if it related to a matter wherein relief or redress could be had only by a judicial proceeding, we do not, after what has been said, deem it necessary to discuss the proposition that the power attempted to be exercised was one confided by the Constitution to the judicial and not to the legislative department of the Government. We think it equally clear that the power asserted is judicial and not legislative.

If, indeed, any purpose had been avowed to impeach the Secretary, the whole aspect of the case would have been changed. But no such purpose is disclosed. None can be inferred from the preamble, and characterization of the conduct of the Secretary by the term improvident, and the absence of any words implying suspicion of criminality, repel the idea of such purpose, for the Secretary could only be impeached for "high crimes and misdemeanors." How could the House of Representatives know, until it had been fairly tried, that the courts were powerless to redress the creditors of J. Cooke & Co. ? The matter was still pending in a court, and what right had the Congress of the United States to interfere with a suit pending in a court of competent jurisdiction ?

Again, what inadequacy of power existed in the court, or, as the preamble assumes, in all courts to give redress which could lawfully be supplied by an investigation by a committee of one house of Congress, or by any act or resolution of Congress on the subject ? The case being one of a judicial nature, for which the powers of the courts usually afford the only remedy, it may well be supposed that those powers were more appropriate, and more efficient in aid of such relief than the powers which belong to a body whose function is exclusively legislative.

If the settlement to which the preamble refers as the principal reason why the courts are rendered powerless was obtained by fraud, or was without authority, or for any conceivable reason could be set aside or avoided, it should be done by some appropriate proceeding in the court which had the whole matter before it, and which had all the power in that case proper to be intrusted to any body, and not by Congress or by any power to be conferred on a committee of one of the two houses.

The resolution adopted as a sequence of this preamble contains no hint of any intention of final action by Congress on the subject. In all the argument of the case no suggestion has been made of what the House of Representatives or the Congress could have done in the way of remedying the wrong or securing the creditors of Jay Cooke & Co., or even the United States. Was it to be simply a fruitless investigation into the personal affairs of individuals ? If so, the House of Representatives had no power or authority in the matter more than any other equal number of gentlemen interested for the government of their country. By "fruitless" we mean that it could result in no valid legislation on the subject to which the inquiry referred.

The supreme court of Pennsylvania, in a well-considered case, reported in Penn. State Reports, vol. 103, p. 486, used the following language:

In considering where the power of removal is lodged, we may draw some light from the interpretation given to the Constitution of the United States. It declares that the President "shall nominate, and by and with the advice and consent of the Senate shall appoint," officers therein named. It is silent on the question of removal of any officer, but declares the judges, both of the supreme and inferior courts, shall hold the offices during good behavior. As to other officers, Congress in 1789 affirmed the right of removal to exist in the President, without any co-operation of the Senate. That view was acquiesced in as the true construction of the Constitution until the passage by Congress of the tenure-of-office act of the 2d of March, 1867, which was superseded by the act of 5th April, 1869, of a modified character. Apart from this legislation, the fact that the consent of the Senate was necessary to authorize the President to appoint, did not prevent him from removing the officers at his pleasure.

Mr. Webster is paraded as an authority to support the present claim of the Senate. In the great debate on "Executive patronage," in 1835, Mr. Webster spoke as follows:

The bill before the Senate, it must be observed, expressly recognizes and admits the actual existence of the power of removal. I do not mean to deny, and the bill does not deny, that at the present moment the President may remove these officers at will, because the early decision adopted that construction, and the laws have since, uniformly, sanctioned it; the law of 1820 expressly affirms the power. I consider it, therefore, a settled point; settled by construction, settled by precedent, settled by the practice of the Government, and settled by statute.

At the same time I am very willing to say that, after considering the question again and again within the last six years, in my deliberate judgment the original decision was wrong. I cannot but think that those who denied the power in 1789 had the best of the argument, and yet I will not say that I know myself so thoroughly as to affirm that this opinion may not have been produced in some measure by that abuse of the power which has been passing before our eyes for several years. It is possible that this experience of the evil may have affected my view of the constitutional argument.

Senator Thurman, in the protracted debate, in 1869, on the bill to repeal the tenure-of-office act, used the following language:

Believing that the original interpretation of the Constitution is the correct one; that the power of removal from office is an executive power; that the duty of exercising that power is enjoined upon the President by the provision of the Constitution that he shall take care that the laws be faithfully executed; believing that the assent of the Senate is not a necessary and logical result that the Senate consents to appointments; believing that no such inference follows from the concurrence of the Senate in making appointments; and believing, also, that it is wiser that it should be as our fathers settled it, that the offices will be better filled and the laws more faithfully executed if this power is vested in the President alone, I feel bound to vote for an unqualified repeal of the tenure-of-office act.

Senator Morton, in the same debate in 1869, spoke as follows:

It was said by the Senator from Illinois that from the beginning men's minds have divided upon the question as to whether this power of removal existed in the Executive absolutely or in connection with the Senate. That the President might exercise it absolutely in the absence of legislation or restriction is confessed by the continued practice of the Government for seventy-eight years, down to 1867.

But the Senator says the minds of men were divided before that time on the question. Sir, that division did not amount to much. There have been very few questions raised in this country that there has not been something said on both sides within the last seventy or eighty years; but there has been as strong a union of opinion in favor of the exercise of this power by the Executive, in the absence of legislation, as can be found, perhaps, upon the exercise of any other power that is granted by the Constitution. Moreover, there has been a great unity of sentiment from the first, that legislation upon that power was not desirable.

My understanding of the tenure-of-office act is that it was adopted for a special purpose; that it was special in its character; that it was intended to meet a condition of things that had never occurred before in the administration, and which we hope will never occur again. It was not made for all future Presidents. Sir, let me ask this question: If the tenure-of-office act had not been passed when it was, and was not now the law of the land, would it enter into the head of any Senator, of any member of Congress, now to pass such a law? The enactment of the law was brought about by a peculiar state of public affairs.

Senator Sherman, in the same debate, in 1869, used the following language:

But now, when we appeal to the Senate to yield to the President the same power of removal that has been exercised by Washington, and every President from Washington down to Johnson, we are referred to old manuscripts that have never been printed before; we are referred to the debates of Webster, and Clay, and Calhoun, &c.

What is the secret of the whole of it? Why, sir, during Washington's administration the anti-Federalists were opposed to Washington, and opposed to his appointing power; they opposed conferring upon Washington the power to remove the Secretary of State. After Washington's administration expired, and John Adams served his fitful four years, with a majority much of the time in both houses against him, where were those gentlemen then with their notions about the power of the President and the power of removal? In the time of Jefferson and Madison and Monroe, where were those gentlemen who were afraid of Executive authority? Did they propose to repeal any of the laws passed in the time of Washington? Not at all. In the time of John Quincy Adams, Mr. Benton made a speech, which has been read. Then John C. Calhoun, who had quarreled with Andrew Jackson, took up the banner of Benton and made Benton's speech over again, and Mr. Webster and Mr. Clay joined in. If there was so much danger of this Executive power, why did not the Democratic party, with a large majority in both Houses, and with a President on their side, repeal these old laws which conferred upon the President the power of removal?

It always has been so, and it always will be so. Notwithstanding all that will be written and said, the *ins* will try to limit the power of the *outs*, and the *outs* will try to limit the power of the *ins*. There is no doubt about it. When the Democrats are in power the Republicans seek to limit their power. When the Republicans are in power the Democrats, on the other hand, seek to limit their power. So it has been in all times, and I do not think we are any wiser or better than our fathers, and probably no worse.

But the crowning indorsement of the settlement of this question by our fathers in 1789, and how it should now be regarded, is contained in the great speech of the distinguished Senator from New York (Mr. Evarts), who always weighs well the full force and meaning of every word he utters. On the impeachment trial of Andrew Johnson (one among other specifications being that he had, without cause, removed Secretary Stanton), Mr. Evarts used the following language:

The Congress of 1789 decided, and its successors for three-quarters of a century acquiesced in that doctrine. I will not weary the Senate with a thorough analysis of the debate of 1789. It is, I believe, decidedly the most important debate in the history of Congress. It is, I think, the best-considered debate in the history of the Government. I think it included among its debaters as many of the able, wise, and learned men, the benefit of whose public service this nation has ever enjoyed, as any debate or measure which this Government has ever had or entertained. The premises in the Constitution were very narrow. The question of removal from office, as a distinct subject, had never occurred to the minds of the men of the convention. The tenure of office was not to be made permanent except in the case of judges of the Supreme Court. The periodicity of Congress, of the Senate, and of the Executive was fixed. Then there was an attribution of the whole interior administrative official powers of the Government to the Executive, with the single qualification, exceptional in itself, that the advice and consent of the Senate should be required as a negative on the President's nomination only.

If on these grounds you dismiss the President from this court convicted and deposed, you dismiss him the victim of the Congress and the martyr of the Constitution by the very terms of your judgment, and you throw open for the masters of us all, in the great debates of an intelligent, instructed, fearless, practical nation of freemen, division of sentiment to shake this country to its center—the omnipotence of Congress as the rallying cry on one side, and the supremacy of the Constitution on the other.

The minority of your committee beg leave to call the attention of the Senate to a few of the most conspicuous and illustrious protests against the wisdom of any attempt by the Senate to usurp the President's power of removal.

Senator Morton, in his speech on the bill to repeal the "Tenure of office act," in 1869, spoke as follows:

What is the effect when the Senate becomes a tribunal for the trial of the causes for which men are suspended? Scarcely any officer can be found of any importance who will not have some Senator upon this floor as his friend, and that Senator will stand up and inquire, "What are the causes for which this man has been suspended? I have known him; he is my friend; perhaps I secured him the appointment, and I cannot consent to his removal unless there is some tangible and sufficient cause made out." Then the Senate must enter upon the investigation. They must examine into the causes of this man's suspension. Is he an honest officer? If not, what has he done? If he is an incapable officer, wherein has he failed? These are questions we must pass upon.

Each one of these suspensions is a case. If we concur in the suspension after examination, the officer goes out of this chamber with a blemish upon his character which he can scarcely outlive. If we refuse to concur in the suspension, we say to the world the President has done this man injustice, either intentionally or unintentionally. If he acted in good faith, he acted in ignorance; if he was well informed, then he acted in bad faith, or out of malicious feelings toward this man.

The President is in some respects on trial also; and as he is to be put on trial, as to whether his judgment has been intelligent, or has been an honest one in regard to the man suspended, he must feel a great deal of interest in the result; and if he is to be adjudged in this way he will hesitate a long time before he makes the suspension. He may be satisfied in his own mind that an officer is not doing right, but unless he can procure facts that are tangible in themselves, and that can be laid definitely before the Senate, or can be stated intelligently before a jury, he will not suspend that man, and the maladministration goes on. Will you tell me, sir, that any administration can be conducted efficiently under the operation of that law?

Now, Mr. President, let me suppose that this law remains in force, what will be the effect of it? When we come back here in the mouth of December, we shall find a long docket of these cases of suspensions, perhaps several hundred of them, and they will have to be tried one by one. We take up the first case. That perhaps takes one afternoon, or one entire executive session; it may be two or three, and I tell you, sir, that this Senate will not have time, if it devotes its whole time to the consideration of these cases, to pass upon them if the President shall suspend every officer that in his judgment ought to be suspended for dishonesty or inefficiency. It will impose upon the Senate a labor that it cannot perform. It will be physically impossible for it to discharge that labor.

There must be responsibility somewhere. The very essence of successful administration under every constitutional government is that the responsibility shall be distinctly located somewhere. Suppose he suspends an officer, and the Senate does not concur in that suspension; that part of the responsibility then belongs to the Senate. It is divided between some sixty or seventy gentlemen on this floor, and the share of each gentleman is very small. If the responsibility is placed between the President and Senate, neither of them will have the whole of it. We divide it up until it amounts to nothing.

Again we quote from the well-considered speech of Senator Sherman in the same debate:

Has the Senator from Vermont arrived at that exemplary and forgiving state of mind that he would not be willing to remove any man who disagreed with him in opinion, or, in other words, who was a Democrat, unless he could be convicted of crime upon satisfactory evidence?

Mr. EDMUNDS. Permit me to ask the Senator whether I ought not to have arrived at that virtuous point on true principles of government, whether I have or not?

Mr. SHERMAN. I do not think so. I believe that all the leading officers of this Government ought to be in harmony with the political sentiments of the majority, and that although the doctrine of Governor Marcy was rather too bluntly stated in his expression that "to the victors belong the spoils," yet in actual practice, in theory, and in fact no administration of this Government ever did or ever will exist without practically acting upon the rule that to the successful party belong the great offices of the Government. It may not be according to the theoretical codes of morality and public policy which the Federalists talked of when the Democrats were in power, and which the Democrats talked of when the Federalists were in power, but still it is a rule of practical administration which will always be applied in a republican form of government.

Now, in my judgment, the tenure-of-office law cannot, with due regard to the public interests, be practically enforced. What has been our experience within two years? When we came back here we were met with piles of documents which the President sent to us; various papers showing that certain officers of the Government had performed acts which in his judgment amounted to misdemeanor, &c., and for which they were suspended. He gave us specific facts and evidence. These cases were referred to the appropriate committees. What were we called upon to examine? We had to take up and carefully read piles of papers and examine each particular case, like a chancellor or a judge of assize. Every suspended officer contended that he was the most innocent man born since the time of Adam. He demanded a trial, and copies of charges and proof and a formal hearing before the committees of this body, he converting us into a court and jury to try his particular case. If we could not try him, why demand charges and evidence?

If the tenure of office act was right in principle we were bound to examine each case to see whether or not the accused officer was, according to the language of the law, guilty of misconduct in office or crime, or had become incapable or legally disqualified. "The result was that some of the committees of this body could not transact their business. These cases were referred, and after great delay were reported upon. In one case the accused was tried, convicted, and sent to the penitentiary while we were deliberating whether he was properly suspended or not." The result was that we did not and could not determine them.

There probably will be from five hundred to five thousand removals during the next year in the service of the United States in the ordinary course of the business of this country. The number of officers to whose appointment the confirmation of this body is required I should estimate in round numbers at from five to twenty thousand. We know there are great multitudes of them whose appointments require the confirmation of the Senate. If we have to remain here, and act upon the cases of all removals, in order to evade the second section, we put ourselves to a great deal of unnecessary trouble merely to evade one of our own laws. If we adjourn, and leave the President without any power to remove, and only the power of suspension, his hands are effectually tied. He can not suspend a postmaster, or a revenue officer, or any of this vast multitude of officers, unless he is prepared upon satisfactory evidence to make out a case of crime or misconduct in office.

It is practically impossible thus to administer the Government. The practical effect of the tenure-of-office act is to keep bad men in office, to divide the responsibility for their misconduct, to enable the President to shield himself from responsibility, and to destroy the energy, efficiency, and unity absolutely necessary in the executive administration of various departments of the Government. That was the practical effect.

Now, Mr. President, look at the actual result as we know it existed. It was the common practice for applicants for office to run here to members of the Senate and say: "I can get an appointment if I am sure of confirmation." There was not a member of the Senate who was not pressed constantly by his constituents to pass his judgment in advance on the question of confirmation and before his appointment— "I can get the appointment if I am sure of confirmation," which reversed the whole order of proceeding in filling the offices of the Government. The Senate became the appointing power; that was the course of business. The result was that many men who had an acute sense of honor, who wished to be free from all this kind of double complication, would not seek or accept office under an administration so hampered and controlled.

S. Rep. 135, pt. 2——2

The duty of the Senate is to advise and consent to appointments. The Constitution confers on this body no power to remove. We consent to removals; we advise as to confirmations. When a man is removed from office, and another name is sent here, we pass simply upon his qualification and fitness for the office; but the Constitution confers upon us no power to proceed in the removal. That is conferred only by the tenure-of office act. Nowhere else do we derive such a power. By the tenure-of-office act the power of removal, as well as the power of confirmation, is conferred on the Senate; and I say with such a power invested in the Senate it will be impossible to avoid controversy and collision between the Executive power and the Senate. We shall share in and finally monopolize the power of the Executive over all the offices of the Government.

Senators must very easily draw distinction between the power of removal and the power of confirmation. The power of confirmation is a resulting power, depending on the previous act of another officer of the Government; and all we say in our act of confirmation is whether or not the person named is a man fit to discharge the duties of the office. That power cannot and will not be abused; but the power of removal is a very different power, a power never contemplated to be invested in the Senate.

It seems to me that we are now acting as judges in our own case. If this great power of the Senate is maintained to prevent the removal of any officer of this Government, it is maintained by the Senate for its own behalf. The public judgment will say that, although we are not nominally interested, we are maintaining powers that were never conferred upon the Senate until two years ago, and which were then conferred for a special purpose. In my opinion we ought to be careful that our judgment should be impartial, and not to be influenced by a love of power.

*   *   *   *   *   *

We share in one-half of the legislative authority of this Government. We are judges over all officers in the trial of impeachment. We participate with the Executive in the power of appointing to office, also in the power to make treaties. I ask if all these great powers are not sufficient for the ambition of any Senate.

*   *   *   *   *   *

As a general rule, it is not wise to mingle the powers of the various departments of the Government. There are three great divisions or departments of the Government that stand apart from each other. They form the triangle of public safety, and upon them rest the safety, order, and good conduct of society. These are the legislative, the executive, and the judicial departments. They have been in exceptional cases mingled. The Senate shares with the President in the appointing power, and also shares with the President in the treaty-making power, &c. It is not wise, in my judgment, to overlook this division of powers.

The foregoing overwhelming array of authorities, reasons, and arguments demonstrate conclusively the far-seeing wisdom and statesmanship of the settlement of the great question now before the Senate by our fathers in 1789. No one had the temerity to disturb it until 1814, during the administration of Mr. Madison.

In the debate in 1835, found in Congressional Debates, vol. 11, part 1, p. 530, Senator Grundy said:

When Mr. Granger, in 1814, was dismissed from the office of Postmaster-General by Mr. Madison, a great sensation was produced both in and out of Congress. This I know, for I was here at that period. Mr. Granger was known to be an able and efficient officer. He was a great favorite with the Democracy of New England. He was not dismissed for any delinquency in the discharge of his public duties. In this state of things the following resolution was introduced into the Senate of the United States, as appears from the second volume, Executive Journal, p. 504. Mr. German submitted the following motion for consideration:

"*Resolved*, That the President of the United States be, and he is hereby, requested to inform the Senate whether the office of Postmaster-General be now vacant, and if vacant, in what manner the same became vacant."

This resolution was rejected by a vote of the Senate, which shows it was the understanding at that time that they had no right to interfere in cases of removal.

This is the only instance, since the decision of the Congress in 1789, in which any member of the Senate has attempted to call on the President for his reasons for removal, until the present Chief Magistrate came into office. In 1830 Mr. Holmes, then a Senator from Maine, introduced a series of resolutions, one of which called for the President's reasons for removals from office, as follows:

Resolved, That the President of the United States be respectfully requested to communicate to the Senate the number, names, and offices of the officers removed by him since the last session of the Senate, with the reasons for each removal.
On motion by Mr. Grundy that said motion be postponed indefinitely, it was determined in the affirmative—yeas 24, nays 21.

The tenure-of-office law, passed in 1867, was the first and only legislative interference by the Senate with the President's power of removal, and the objects and exceptional reasons of that act of usurpation have been fully explained by those who aided in its passage. President Grant, in his first annual message in 1869, recommended the total repeal of the tenure-of-office law, for the reason that it would be impossible for him to administer the Government under its operation. The House, by nearly a unanimous vote, recommended the repeal.

The House bill was amended in the Senate as now found in sections 1767 and 1768. Section 1767 is part of the original act, with the material qualification that it is subjected to the control of section 1768. Section 1768 is the controlling part of the whole act as it now exists. That section provides that—

During any recess of the Senate, the President is authorized, in his discretion, to suspend any civil officer appointed by and with the advice and consent of the Senate, until the end of the next session of the Senate, and to designate some suitable person, subject to be removed, in his discretion, by the designation of another, to perform the duties of such suspended officer in the mean time ; and the person so designated shall take the oath and give the bond required by law to be taken and given by the suspended officer, and shall, during the time he performs the duties of such office, be entitled to the salary and emoluments of the office, no part of which shall belong to the officer suspended. The President shall, within thirty days after the commencement of each session of the Senate, except for any office which in his opinion ought not to be filled, nominate persons to fill all vacancies in office which existed at the meeting of the Senate, whether temporarily filled or not, and also in the place of all officers suspended ; and if the Senate during such session shall refuse to advise and consent to an appointment in the place of any suspended officer, then, and not otherwise, the President shall nominate another person as soon as practicable to the same session of the Senate for the office.

It must be conceded, as this section expressly provides, that the President's power to suspend a civil officer in vacations of the Senate is "discretionary," and that such suspended officer remains out of the office at least until the Senate adjourns, when he is again certainly liable to be suspended if reinstated by the operation of section 1768, which is denied by many of the best lawyers in the Senate, and so on, without limitation as to time, or discretion, should the President elect to exercise his power of suspension. On this discretionary power of the President to suspend, as called in the statute, or to remove from office, under the Constitution, the Supreme Court of the United States, in the case of Marbury *vs.* Madison, 1 Cranch's Reports, at p. 165, says:

By the Constitution of the United States the President is invested with certain important political powers, in the exercise of which he is to use his own discretion, and is accountable only to his country in his political character and to his own conscience. To aid him in the performance of these duties he is authorized to appoint certain officers, who act by his authority, and in conformity with his orders.
In such cases their acts are his acts, and whatever opinion may be entertained of the manner in which executive discretion may be used, still there exists, and can exist, no power to control that discretion. The subjects are political. They respect the nation, not individual rights, and being intrusted to the Executive, the decision of the Executive is conclusive.

In relation to the exercise by the President of his power of suspension or removal for cause, the distinguished Senator from Vermont (Mr.

Edmunds), in the debate on the bill to repeal the tenure-of-office act, used the following language in answer to Senator Morton:

I say with him that the President of the United States has no business to nominate to us a man—I am now speaking of moral business, because the Constitution gives him a right to nominate as often as he pleases—the President has no right to propose to us to put out one man and put in another, unless there is cause. Now, what is cause? The Constitution has made the cause. The united discretion of the President of the United States and the representatives of the States, that is cause. If the President of the United States thinks for any reason that satisfies his moral nature that it is better to make a change in an office, and proposes it to us, and we are satisfied for any reason that is consonant to our moral sense of right and wrong that that change ought to or may be made, then it is done, and there is cause. My friend may go into a dissertation if he wishes to do so, when it comes to his turn to speak, upon proximate and final cause. There is ever so much discussion in books of philosophy about that.

But it is cause enough for me, sir, constitutional cause, if the Senator will, when the President of the United States acting, if he is honest, as he always must, upon a conscientious regard for the public service and a conscientious sense of his responsibility to the people and to God, chooses to send in one man's name for a place that another man holds. When he has done that he has done his duty, whether that cause satisfies my friend and me or not. Then it becomes our opportunity to speak and to consider, and if we are satisfied with the cause, or with any other cause that appeals to our judgment and good sense, the act is accomplished.

We have in this extract the key to the report of the majority of your committee.

The Senator from Vermont, the able chairman of the Judiciary Committee, is entitled to the distinction of being the author of the remarkable discovery that the unqualified, exclusive, and independent power of removing or suspending officers of the United States can be conceded to the President for his free exercise for any cause or reason that may satisfy him, and that the Senate has no right to interfere with or control, in any manner, the use of such power by the President; but that after the President has so exercised his power, and made the suspension for any cause satisfactory to him, and nominates to the Senate a person to take the place of the suspended officer, then the power of the Senate intervenes to "advise and consent to the nomination," which is just as absolute, exclusive, and independent as the President's power to suspend and nominate, and that in the exercise of this power the Senate can decide, with or without cause, or for any cause satisfactory to them, to withhold their advice and consent to the nomination.

The soundness of this proposition may be admitted, as the Senate can arbitrarily exercise any discretionary power; but it leaves the question unanswered whether the Senate has any constitutional or lawful right to request the President or direct the Attorney-General to transmit to the Senate, in executive session, papers and documents in the keeping of either, that relate exclusively to suspensions by the President under section 1768 of the tenure-of-office act. Such papers and documents have no existence or character as public documents. They relate solely to a matter under the absolute power and control of the President, "in the exercise of which," in the language of the Supreme Court, "he is to use his own discretion, and is accountable only to his country in his political character and to his own conscience."

The right of the Senate or House to papers and documents in the keeping of the President or the heads of Departments must be decided by their contents and character and the use that can be made of them in the exercise of any power or jurisdiction intrusted to either house by the Constitution in executive or legislative session. If the papers and documents can instruct or aid either house in the exercise of legislative or executive powers or privileges intrusted to them by the Constitution, the right of either house to the possession of such papers or documents, or their contents, has never been questioned. It is impossible, in the judgment of the minority, for the majority or for the Senate to find the slightest support, excuse, or justification for their claim to the papers and documents relating exclusively to suspensions by the President, except on the ground that the Senate has the same power under the Constitution of advising and consenting to suspensious by the President that they have to advise and consent to his appointments.

There is no ingenuity sufficiently skilled in special pleading to separate the two powers of suspension and appointment, and make each absolute and independent of the other, and at the same time claim that the custodian of one power is entitled to all the papers and documents in the sole keeping of the custodian of the other power, and relating exclusively to matters within his jurisdiction.

But it is insisted that the President has no right to know or to inquire what use the Senate intends making of the papers and documents. Can it be seriously urged that if the papers and documents called for are not public, but private, and relate exclusively to the official acts of the President, for which he is under no responsibility to the Senate, the Senate has any right to their possession? Who is to judge whether the papers and documents are public or private, the President, who knows their contents and to what they relate, or the Senate, who has no such information? How is the Senate to pass on the character and contents of the papers and documents before seeing them, and how will it be if after inspection of the papers and documents the Senate decides it has no right to their possession? How can the President possibly avoid knowing what use the Senate intends making of the papers when they show on their face that they cannot be made to relate to anything but suspension? And if it were possible for the President to close his eyes to the contents of the papers and documents, and the use that is to be made of them by the Senate, can the right be denied to those Senators who resist the claim of the Senate to have inspection of papers and documents relating exclusively to suspensions by the President, to know what use is intended to be made of the papers and documents by the Senate?

The minority claim to know what use is intended to be made by the majority of your committee of the papers and documents called for and relating exclusively to suspensions; and with that knowledge the minority are satisfied that their possession and use by the Senate is unconstitutional and supported by no law, usage, or public policy, and that their transmission to the Senate was rightfully refused by the Attorney-General on the order of the President. The minority of your committee cannot close their report without expressing surprise at the appearance in the majority report of the following resolution:

Resolved, That the provision of section 1754 of the Revised Statutes declaring—
"That persons honorably discharged from the military or naval service by reason of disability resulting from wounds or sickness incurred in the line of duty shall be preferred for appointments to civil offices, provided they are found to possess the business capacity necessary for the proper discharge of the duties of such office, ought to be faithfully and fully put in execution, and that to remove, or to propose to remove, any such soldier whose faithfulness, competency, and character are above reproach, and to give place to another who has not rendered such service, is a violation of the spirit of the law, and of the practical gratitude the people and Government of the United States owe to the defenders of constitutional liberty and the integrity of the Government."

Under what action of the Senate does the majority claim the authority to report such a resolution to the Senate for its adoption? What possible connection has the subject mentioned in the resolution with the papers and documents called for in the case of the suspension of Duskin, which is the only matter referred by the Senate to the Judiciary Committee? The information of the minority of your committee is that Duskin never was a Union soldier, but, on the contrary, was either a member of the Confederate army or a Confederate sympathizer in his native State of North Carolina.

The minority of your committee fully indorse section 1754 of the Revised Statutes, and heartily favor its faithful execution; but their information and belief satisfy them that under its operation during the administrations of Republican Presidents partisan and political influences and considerations have governed in a great degree in the selection of the intended beneficiaries of that statute, so that no equal and just distribution has been made by Republican Presidents among the meritorious class described in the law, as is doubtless desired alike by Republican and Democratic soldiers and marines who were comrades in a common cause.

Such unauthorized action of the majority of your committee serves one purpose, and that is to furnish additional proof of what was before manifest, that the object and intent of this extraordinary proceeding is to secure political and partisan advantage and benefit. The inevitable result is to arraign President Cleveland and try him by the Senate, with an unfriendly political majority, for making suspensions in alleged violation of his public pledges and promises not to make removals or suspensions except for cause.

President Cleveland's promises and pledges are part of the published history of the country, and for their faithful performance he denies his responsibility to the Senate, and stands ready for trial by the people. He did make the promise that during the term of a civil officer he would not suspend or remove him for the *sole reason* that he was a Republican. *Merely being a Republican*, if he had been, and was a capable, faithful, and efficient officer, the President declared he would not regard as sufficient cause. But if such officer, *while in office*, had used its power or influence or emoluments to promote the organization and success of his party, by attending county, district, State, or national conventions, and making himself active as a partisan in elections, the President has publicly declared such conduct and action by any incumbent, however capable, faithful, and efficient in the discharge of his official duties, as a violation of the spirit of the law declaring that civil office is a public trust for public uses, and not to be employed as an element of power in party organizations and elections, and that such conduct would be treated as sufficient cause for suspensions.

The President declines to submit voluntarily to the decision of a tribunal, having no jurisdiction over the question, the sufficiency of such cause for suspensions—especially when his fear is that such conduct in the officer might be regarded by the Republican majority as a reason for the retention of the incumbent in office. The President will never avoid a trial by the people for the exercise of any of his powers or the discharge of any of his official duties, as he will have a fair tribunal on the whole truth. But he declines obedience to any unlawful summons to trial under usurped authority by an unfriendly tribunal on mere papers and documents relating exclusively to suspensions, and containing in nearly every case only a partial statement of the causes, facts, and reasons for his official act of suspension. In a large majority of the cases

of suspension, as the minority are informed, the President had information communicated to him orally by persons considered reliable, which
it would be impossible for him to remember or reproduce in every case,
so as to put the Senate in possession of all the facts which governed him
in the suspension, if the Senate had the authority under the Constitution or laws of the United States to call him to an account.

In conclusion, the minority of your committee are gratified at being
able to state that in the Forty-sixth Congress, when the Democrats
had a majority in the Senate, no such spectacle as that now exhibited
to the country was ever witnessed in the history of its proceedings.

All of which is respectfully submitted.

> JAMES L. PUGH.
> RICHARD COKE.
> GEORGE G. VEST.
> HOWELL E. JACKSON.

www.ingramcontent.com/pod-product-compliance
Lightning Source LLC
Chambersburg PA
CBHW021552270326
41931CB00009B/1180